Coaching Youth Hockey

Second Edition

American Sport Education Program

Human Kinetics

Library of Congress Cataloging-in-Publication Data

Coaching youth hockey / American Sport Education Program.--2nd ed.
  p. cm.
  ISBN 0-7360-3795-0
  1. Hockey--Coaching. 2. Roller hockey. I. American Sport Education Program.

  GV848.25 .C63 2001
  796.962'07'7--dc21

                        2001016873

ISBN-10: 0-7360-3795-0
ISBN-13: 978-0-7360-3795-2

Acquisitions Editor: Russell Medbery PhD; **Games Consultant:** Larry Lauer; **Managing Editor:** Wendy McLaughlin; **Assistant Editor:** Dan Brachtesende; **Copyeditor:** Jan Feeney; **Proofreader:** Sue Fetters; **Graphic Designer:** Fred Starbird; **Graphic Artist:** Tara Welsch; **Photo Manager:** Gayle Garrison; **Cover Designer:** Jack W. Davis; **Photographer (cover):** ©Sportschrome; **Photographer (interior):** Tom Roberts; **Art Manager:** Craig Newsom; **Illustrators:** Tom Janowski, Roberto Sabas, and Tim Offenstein; **Printer:** United Graphics

Material in chapters 4 and 6 are used, by permission, of YMCA of the USA *Coaching YMCA Winners Baseball and Softball,* 1999, (Champaign, IL: Human Kinetics).

Copies of this book are available at special discounts for bulk purchase for sales promotions, premiums, fund-raising, or educational use. Special editions or book excerpts can also be created to specifications. For details, contact the Special Sales Manager at Human Kinetics.

Printed in the United States of America   10 9 8 7 6 5 4

Human Kinetics
Web site: www.HumanKinetics.com

United States: Human Kinetics, P.O. Box 5076, Champaign, IL 61825-5076
800-747-4457
e-mail: humank@hkusa.com

Canada: Human Kinetics, 475 Devonshire Road Unit 100, Windsor, ON N8Y 2L5
800-465-7301 (in Canada only)
e-mail: orders@hkcanada.com

Europe: Human Kinetics, 107 Bradford Road, Stanningley, Leeds LS28 6AT
United Kingdom
+44 (0)113 255 5665
e-mail: hk@hkeurope.com

Australia: Human Kinetics, 57A Price Avenue, Lower Mitcham, South Australia 5062
08 8372 0999
e-mail: liaw@hkaustralia.com

New Zealand: Human Kinetics, Division of Sports Distributors NZ Ltd.
P.O. Box 300 226 Albany, North Shore City, Auckland
0064 9 448 1207
e-mail: info@humankinetics.co.nz

Contents

Welcome to Coaching!

Coaching young people is an exciting way to be involved in sport. But it isn't easy. Some coaches are overwhelmed by the responsibilities involved in helping athletes through their early sport experiences. And that's not surprising, because coaching youngsters requires more than bringing the pucks and sticks to the rink and letting them play. It involves preparing them physically and mentally to compete effectively, fairly, and safely in their sport, and providing them with a positive role model.

This book will help you meet the challenges *and* experience the many rewards of coaching young athletes. In this book you'll learn how to meet your responsibilities as a coach, communicate well and provide for safety, use a highly effective method – the games approach – to teaching tactics and skills, and learn strategies for coaching on game day. We also provide three sets of season plans to guide you throughout your season.

This book serves as a text for ASEP's Coaching Youth Sport course. If you would like more information about this course or other ASEP courses and resources, please contact us at

ASEP
P.O. Box 5076
Champaign, IL 61825-5076
1-800-747-5698

www.asep.com

chapter 1

Stepping Into Coaching

If you are like most youth league coaches, you have probably been recruited from the ranks of concerned parents, sport enthusiasts, or community volunteers. Like many rookie and veteran coaches, you probably have had little formal instruction on how to coach. But when the call went out for coaches to assist with the local youth hockey program, you answered because you like children and enjoy hockey, and perhaps because you wanted to be involved in a worthwhile community activity.

Your initial coaching assignment may be difficult. Like many volunteers, you may not know everything there is to know about hockey or about how to work with children. Coaching Youth Hockey will help you learn the basics of coaching hockey effectively.

To start, let's take a look at what's involved in being a coach. What are your responsibilities? We'll also talk about how to handle the situation when your child is on the team you coach, and we'll examine five tools for being an effective coach.

Your Responsibilities As a Coach

As a hockey coach, you'll be called upon to do the following:

1. **Provide a safe physical environment.** Playing hockey holds an inherent risk, but as a coach you're responsible for regularly inspecting the practice and competition rinks (see the checklists for facilities, equipment, and support personnel in chapter 6).

2. **Communicate in a positive way.** You'll communicate not only with your players but also with parents, officials, and administrators. Communicate in a way that is positive and that demonstrates you have the best interests of the players at heart. Chapter 2 will help you communicate effectively and positively.

3. **Teach the tactics and skills of hockey.** We'll show you an innovative "games approach" to teaching and practicing the tactics and skills young athletes need to know—an approach that kids thoroughly enjoy. We ask you to help all players be the best they can be. In chapter 5 we'll show you how to teach hockey skills, and in chapter 9 we'll provide season plans for 8- to 9-year-olds, 10- to 11-year-olds, and 12- to 14-year-olds, respectively. In chapter 8 we'll provide descriptions of all the skills you'll need to teach and to help you detect and correct errors that players typically make.

4. **Teach the rules of hockey.** We'll ask you to teach your players the rules of hockey. You'll find the rules in chapter 7.

5. **Direct players in competition.** This includes determining starting lineups and a substitution plan, relating appropriately to officials and to opposing coaches and players, and making tactical decisions during games (see chapter 6). Remember that the focus is not on winning at all costs, but in coaching your kids to compete well, do their best, and strive to win within the rules.

6. **Help your players become fit and value fitness for a lifetime.** We want you to help your players be fit so they can play hockey safely and successfully. We also want your players to learn to become fit on their own, understand the value of fitness, and enjoy training. Thus, we ask you not to make them do push-ups or run laps for punishment. Make it fun to get fit for hockey, and make it fun to play hockey so they'll stay fit for a lifetime.

7. **Help young people develop character.** Character development includes learning caring, honesty, respect, and responsibility. These in-

tangible qualities are no less important to teach than the skill of shooting the puck well. We ask you to teach these values to players both by conducting Team Circles after every game and by demonstrating and encouraging behaviors that express these values at all times.

These are your responsibilities as a coach. But coaching becomes even more complicated when your child is a player on the team you coach. If this is the case, you'll have to take into account your roles as both a coach and a parent, and think about how those roles relate to each other.

Coaching Your Own Child

Many coaches are parents, but the two roles should not be confused. Unlike your role as a parent, as a coach you are responsible not only to yourself and your child, but also to the organization, all the players on the team (including your child), and their parents. Because of this additional responsibility, your behavior on the hockey rink will be different from your behavior at home, and your son or daughter may not understand why.

For example, imagine the confusion of a young boy who is the center of his parents' attention at home but is barely noticed by his father/coach in the sport setting. Or consider the mixed signals received by a young girl whose hockey skill is constantly evaluated by a mother/coach who otherwise rarely comments on her daughter's activities. You need to explain to your son or daughter your new responsibilities and how they will affect your relationship when coaching.

Take the following steps to avoid problems in coaching your child:

- Ask your child if he or she wants you to coach the team.
- Explain why you wish to be involved with the team.
- Discuss with your child how your interactions will change when you take on the role of coach at practices or games.
- Limit your coaching behavior to when you are in the coaching role.
- Avoid parenting during practice or game situations, to keep your role clear in your child's mind.
- Reaffirm your love for your child, irrespective of his or her performance on the hockey rink.

Now let's look at some of the qualities that will help you become an effective coach.

Five Tools of an Effective Coach

Have you purchased the traditional coaching tools—things like whistles, coaching clothes, skates, and a clipboard? They'll help you coach, but to be a successful coach you'll need five other tools that cannot be bought. These tools are available only through self-examination and hard work; they're easy to remember with the acronym COACH:

C – Comprehension

O – Outlook

A – Affection

C – Character

H – Humor

Comprehension

Comprehension of the rules, tactics, and skills of hockey is required. You must understand the basic elements of the sport. To assist you in learning about the game, we describe rules, tactics, and skills in chapters 7 and 8. We also provide season plans in chapter 9.

To improve your comprehension of hockey, take the following steps:

- Read the sport-specific section of this book in chapters 7, 8, and 9.
- Consider reading other hockey coaching books, including those available from the American Sport Education Program (ASEP).
- Contact youth hockey organizations.
- Attend hockey clinics.
- Talk with more experienced coaches.
- Observe local college, high school, and youth hockey games.
- Watch hockey games on television.

In addition to having hockey knowledge, you must implement proper training and safety methods so your players can participate with little risk of injury. Even then, injuries may occur. And more often than not, you'll be the first person responding to your players' injuries, so be sure you understand the basic emergency care procedures described in chapter 3. Also, read in that chapter how to handle more serious sport injury situations.

Outlook

This coaching tool refers to your perspective and goals—what you are seeking as a coach. The most common coaching objectives are to (a) have fun, (b) help players develop their physical, mental, and social skills, and (c) win. Thus your outlook involves the priorities you set, your planning, and your vision for the future.

While all coaches focus on competition, we want you to focus on positive competition, keeping the pursuit of victory in perspective by making decisions that first are in the best interest of the players, and second will help to win the game.

So how do you know if your outlook and priorities are in order? Here's a little test for you:

Which situation would you be most proud of?
   a. Knowing that each participant enjoyed playing hockey.
   b. Seeing that all players improved their hockey skills.
   c. Winning the league championship.

Which statement best reflects your thoughts about sport?
   a. If it isn't fun, don't do it.
   b. Everyone should learn something every day.
   c. Sport isn't fun if you don't win.

How would you like your players to remember you?
   a. As a coach who was fun to play for.
   b. As a coach who provided a good base of fundamental skills.
   c. As a coach who had a winning record.

Which would you most like to hear a parent of a player on your team say?
   a. Mike really had a good time playing hockey this year.
   b. Nicole learned some important lessons playing hockey this year.
   c. Willie played on the first-place hockey team this year.

Which of the following would be the most rewarding moment of your season?
   a. Having your team not want to stop playing, even after practice is over.

b. Seeing one of your players finally master the skill of stick handling without constantly looking at the puck/ball.

c. Winning the league championship.

Look over your answers. If you most often selected "a" responses, then having fun is most important to you. A majority of "b" answers suggests that skill development is what attracts you to coaching. And if "c" was your most frequent response, winning is tops on your list of coaching priorities. If your priorities are in order, your players' well-being will take precedence over your team's win-loss record every time.

The American Sport Education Program (ASEP) has a motto that will help you keep your outlook in line with the best interests of the kids on your team. It summarizes in four words all you need to remember when establishing your coaching priorities:

Athletes First, Winning Second

This motto recognizes that striving to win is an important, even vital, part of sports. But it emphatically states that no efforts in striving to win should be made at the expense of the athletes' well-being, development, and enjoyment.

Take the following actions to better define your outlook:

1. Determine your priorities for the season.
2. Prepare for situations that challenge your priorities.
3. Set goals for yourself and your players that are consistent with those priorities.
4. Plan how you and your players can best attain those goals.
5. Review your goals frequently to be sure that you are staying on track.

Affection

This is another vital tool you will want to have in your coaching kit: a genuine concern for the young people you coach. It involves having a love for kids, a desire to share with them your love and knowledge of hockey, and the patience and understanding that allow each individual playing for you to grow from his or her involvement in sport.

You can demonstrate your affection and patience in many ways, including these:

⊙ Make an effort to get to know each player on your team.
⊙ Treat each player as an individual.

- Empathize with players trying to learn new and difficult skills.
- Treat players as you would like to be treated under similar circumstances.
- Be in control of your emotions.
- Show your enthusiasm for being involved with your team.
- Keep an upbeat and positive tone in all of your communications.

Character

The fact that you have decided to coach young hockey players probably means that you think participation in sport is important. But whether or not that participation develops character in your players depends as much on you as it does on the sport itself. How can you build character in your players?

Having good character means modeling appropriate behaviors for sport and life. That means more than just saying the right things. What you say and what you do must match. There is no place in coaching for the "Do as I say, not as I do" philosophy. Challenge, support, encourage, and reward every youngster, and your players will be more likely to accept, even celebrate, their differences. Be in control before, during, and after all practices and contests. And don't be afraid to admit that you were wrong. No one is perfect!

Consider the following steps to being a good role model:

- Take stock of your strengths and weaknesses.
- Build on your strengths.
- Set goals for yourself to improve upon those areas you would not like to see copied.
- If you slip up, apologize to your team and to yourself. You'll do better next time.

Humor

Humor is an often-overlooked coaching tool. For our use it means having the ability to laugh at yourself and with your players during practices and contests. Nothing helps balance the tone of a serious skill-learning session like a chuckle or two. And a sense of humor puts in perspective the many mistakes your players will make. So don't get upset over each miscue or respond negatively to erring players. Allow your players and yourself to enjoy the ups, and don't dwell on the downs.

Here are some tips for injecting humor into your practices:

- Make practices fun by including a variety of activities.
- Keep all players involved in games and skill practices.
- Consider laughter by your players a sign of enjoyment, not of waning discipline.
- Smile!

Communicating As a Coach

In chapter 1 you learned about the tools needed to COACH: Comprehension, Outlook, Affection, Character, and Humor. These are essentials for effective coaching; without them, you'd have a difficult time getting started. But none of the tools will work if you don't know how to use them with your athletes — and this requires skillful communication. This chapter examines what communication is and how you can become a more effective communicator-coach.

What's Involved in Communication?

Coaches often mistakenly believe that communication involves only instructing players to do something, but verbal commands are only a small part of the communication process. More than half of what is communicated is nonverbal. So remember when you are coaching: Actions speak louder than words.

Communication in its simplest form involves two people: a sender and a receiver. The sender transmits the message verbally, through facial expressions, and possibly through body language. Once the message is sent, the receiver must assimilate it successfully. A receiver who fails to attend or listen will miss parts, if not all, of the message.

How Can I Send More Effective Messages?

Young athletes often have little understanding of the rules and skills of hockey and probably even less confidence in playing it. So they need accurate, understandable, and supportive messages to help them along. That's why your verbal and nonverbal messages are so important.

Verbal Messages

"Sticks and stones may break my bones, but words will never hurt me" isn't true. Spoken words can have a strong and long-lasting effect. And coaches' words are particularly influential because youngsters place great importance on what coaches say. Perhaps you, like many former youth sport participants, have a difficult time remembering much of anything you were told by your elementary school teachers, but you can still recall several specific things your coaches at that level said to you. Such is the lasting effect of a coach's comments to a player.

Whether you are correcting misbehavior, teaching a player how to hit the puck/ball, or praising a player for good effort, you should consider a number of things when sending a message verbally. They include the following:

- Be positive and honest.
- State it clearly and simply.
- Say it loud enough, and say it again.
- Be consistent.

Be Positive and Honest

Nothing turns people off like hearing someone nag all the time, and athletes react similarly to a coach who gripes constantly. Kids particularly need encouragement because they often doubt their ability to perform in a sport. So look for and tell your players what they did well.

But don't cover up poor or incorrect play with rosy words of praise. Kids know all too well when they've erred, and no cheerfully expressed cliche can undo their mistakes. If you fail to acknowledge players' errors, your athletes will think you are a phony.

A good way to correct a performance error is to first point out what the athlete did correctly. Then explain in a positive way what he or she is doing wrong and show him or her how to correct it. Finish by encouraging the athlete and emphasizing the correct performance.

Be sure not to follow a positive statement with the word but. For example, don't say, "That was good location on your pass, Kelly. But if you follow through with your stick until it is pointing at the target, you'll get a little more zip on the puck." Saying it this way causes many kids to ignore the positive statement and focus on the negative one. Instead, say something like "That was good location on your pass, Kelly. And if you follow through with your stick until it is pointing at the target, you'll get a little more zip on the puck. That was right on target. That's the way to go."

State It Clearly and Simply

Positive and honest messages are good, but only if expressed directly in words your players understand. "Beating around the bush" is ineffective and inefficient. And if you do ramble, your players will miss the point of your message and probably lose interest. Here are some tips for saying things clearly:

- Organize your thoughts before speaking to your athletes.
- Explain things thoroughly, but don't bore them with long-winded monologues.
- Use language your players can understand. However, avoid trying to be hip by using their age group's slang vocabulary.

Say It Loud Enough, and Say It Again

Talk to your team in a voice that all members can hear and interpret. A crisp, vigorous voice commands attention and respect; garbled and weak speech is tuned out. It's OK, in fact, appropriate, to soften your voice when speaking to a player individually about a personal problem. But most of the time your messages will be for all your players to hear, so make sure they can! An enthusiastic voice also motivates players and tells them you enjoy being their coach. A word of caution, however: Don't dominate the setting with a booming voice that distracts attention from players' performances.

Sometimes what you say, even if stated loudly and clearly, won't sink in the first time. This may be particularly true when young athletes hear words they don't understand. To avoid boring repetition and yet still get your message across, say the same thing in a slightly different way. For instance, you might first tell your players, "In a one-on-one situation on defense, keep your body between your opponent and the net." Soon afterward, remind them, "In a one-on-one situation on defense, watch your opponent's stomach rather than the puck and force the player to the outside." The second form of the message may get through to players who missed it the first time around.

Be Consistent

People often say things in ways that imply a different message. For example, a touch of sarcasm added to the words "Way to go!" sends an entirely different message than the words themselves suggest. Avoid sending such mixed messages. Keep the tone of your voice consistent with the words you use. And don't say something one day and contradict it the next; players will get their wires crossed.

Nonverbal Messages

Just as you should be consistent in the tone of voice and words you use, you should also keep your verbal and nonverbal messages consistent. An extreme example of failing to do this would be shaking your head, indicating disapproval, while at the same time telling a player "Nice try." Which is the player to believe, your gesture or your words?

Messages can be sent nonverbally in a number of ways. Facial expressions and body language are just two of the more obvious forms of nonverbal signals that can help you when you coach.

Facial Expressions

The look on a person's face is the quickest clue to what he or she thinks or feels. Your players know this, so they will study your face, looking for any sign that will tell them more than the words you say. Don't try to fool them by putting on a happy or blank "mask." They'll see through it, and you'll lose credibility.

Serious, stone-faced expressions are no help to kids who need cues as to how they are performing. They will just assume you're unhappy or disinterested. Don't be afraid to smile. A smile from a coach can give a great boost to an unsure athlete. Plus, a smile lets your players know that you are happy coaching them. But don't overdo it, or your players won't be able to tell when you are genuinely pleased by something they've done or when you are just putting on a smiling face.

Body Language

What would your players think you were feeling if you came to practice slouched over, with your head down and shoulders slumped? Tired? Bored? Unhappy? What would they think you were feeling if you watched them during a contest with your hands on your hips, your jaws clenched, and your face reddened? Upset with them? Disgusted at an official? Mad at a fan?

Probably some or all of these things would enter your players' minds. And none of these impressions is the kind you want your players to have of you. That's why you should carry yourself in a pleasant, confident, and vigorous manner. Such a posture not only projects happiness with your coaching role but also provides a good example for your young players, who may model your behavior.

Physical contact can also be a very important use of body language. A handshake, a pat on the head, an arm around the shoulder, or even a big hug are effective ways of showing approval, concern, affection, and joy to your players. Youngsters are especially in need of this type of nonverbal message. Keep within the obvious moral and legal limits, of course, but don't be reluctant to touch your players, sending a message that can only truly be expressed in that way.

How Can I Improve My Receiving Skills?

Now, let's examine the other half of the communication process — receiving messages. Too often very good senders are very poor receivers of messages. But as a coach of young athletes, you must be able to fulfill both roles effectively.

The requirements for receiving messages are quite simple, but receiving skills are perhaps less satisfying and therefore underdeveloped compared to sending skills. People seem to naturally enjoy hearing themselves talk more than hearing others talk. But if you read about the keys to receiving messages and make a strong effort to use them with your players, you'll be surprised by what you've been missing.

Attention!

First, you must pay attention; you must want to hear what others have to communicate to you. That's not always easy when you're busy coaching and have many things competing for your attention. But in one-on-one or team meetings with players, you must really focus on what they are telling you, both verbally and nonverbally. You'll be amazed at the little signals you pick up. Not only will such focused attention help you

catch every word your players say, but also you'll notice your players' moods and physical states. In addition, you'll get an idea of your players' feelings toward you and other players on the team.

Listen CARE-FULLY

How we receive messages from others, perhaps more than anything else we do, demonstrates how much we care for the sender and what that person has to tell us. If you care little for your players or have little regard for what they have to say, it will show in how you attend and listen to them. Check yourself. Do you find your mind wandering to what you are going to do after practice while one of your players is talking to you? Do you frequently have to ask your players, "What did you say?" If so, you need to work on your receiving mechanics of attending and listening. But perhaps the most critical question you should ask yourself, if you find that you're missing the messages your players send, is this: Do I care?

Providing Feedback

So far we've discussed separately the sending and receiving of messages. But we all know that senders and receivers switch roles several times during an interaction. One person initiates a communication by sending a message to another person, who then receives the message. The receiver then switches roles and becomes the sender by responding to the person who sent the initial message. These verbal and nonverbal responses are called feedback.

Your players will be looking to you for feedback all the time. They will want to know how you think they are performing, what you think of their ideas, and whether their efforts please you. Obviously, you can respond in many different ways. How you respond will strongly affect your players. They will respond most favorably to positive feedback.

Praising players when they have performed or behaved well is an effective way of getting them to repeat (or try to repeat) that behavior in the future. And positive feedback for effort is an especially effective way to motivate youngsters to work on difficult skills. So rather than shouting and providing negative feedback to players who have made mistakes, try offering players positive feedback, letting them know what they did correctly and how they can improve.

Sometimes just the way you word feedback can make it more positive than negative. For example, instead of saying, "Don't shoot the puck that way," you might say, "Shoot the puck this way." Then your players will be focusing on what to do instead of what not to do.

You can give positive feedback verbally and nonverbally. Telling a player, especially in front of teammates, that he or she has performed well is a great way to boost the confidence of a youngster. And a pat on the back or a handshake can be a very tangible way of communicating your recognition of a player's performance.

Who Else Do I Need to Communicate With?

Coaching involves not only sending and receiving messages and providing proper feedback to players, but also interacting with parents, fans, game officials, and opposing coaches. If you don't communicate effectively with these groups of people, your coaching career will be unpleasant and short-lived. So try the following suggestions for communicating with these groups.

Parents

A player's parents need to be assured that their son or daughter is under the direction of a coach who is both knowledgeable about the sport and concerned about the youngster's well-being. You can put their worries to rest by holding a preseason parent-orientation meeting in which you describe your background and your approach to coaching.

If parents contact you with a concern during the season, listen to them closely and try to offer positive responses. If you need to communicate with parents, catch them after a practice, give them a phone call, or send a note through the mail. Messages sent to parents through players are too often lost, misinterpreted, or forgotten.

Fans

The stands probably won't be overflowing at your contests, but that only means that you'll more easily hear the few fans who criticize your coaching. When you hear something negative said about the job you're doing, don't respond. Keep calm, consider whether the message had any value, and if not, forget it. Acknowledging critical, unwarranted comments from a fan during a contest will only encourage others to voice their opinions. So put away your "rabbit ears" and communicate to fans, through your actions, that you are a confident, competent coach.

Prepare your players for fans' criticisms. Tell them it is you, not the spectators, they should listen to. If you notice that one of your players is rattled by a fan's comment, reassure the player that your evaluation is more objective and favorable—and the one that counts.

Game Officials

How you communicate with officials will have a great influence on the way your players behave toward them. Therefore, you need to set an example. Greet officials with a handshake, an introduction, and perhaps some casual conversation about the upcoming contest. Indicate your respect for them before, during, and after the contest. Don't make nasty remarks, shout, or use disrespectful body gestures. Your players will see you do it, and they'll get the idea that such behavior is appropriate. Plus, if the official hears or sees you, the communication between the two of you will break down.

Opposing Coaches

Make an effort to visit with the coach of the opposing team before the game. During the game, don't get into a personal feud with the opposing coach. Remember, it's the kids, not the coaches, who are competing. And by getting along well with the opposing coach, you'll show your players that competition involves cooperation.

Providing for Players' Safety

One of your players breaks free down the rink, skating toward the goal. But out of nowhere races a defender who catches up with and accidentally trips up the goal-bound player. You see that your player is not getting up from the ground and seems to be in pain. What do you do?

No coach wants to see players get hurt. But injury remains a reality of sport participation; consequently, you must be prepared to provide first aid when injuries occur and to protect yourself against unjustified lawsuits. Fortunately, there are many preventive measures coaches can institute to reduce the risk. In this chapter we describe

- ⊙ steps you can take to prevent injuries,
- ⊙ first aid and emergency responses for when injuries occur, and
- ⊙ your legal responsibilities as a coach.

The Game Plan for Safety

You can't prevent all injuries from happening, but you can take preventive measures that give your players the best possible chance for injury-free participation. In creating the safest possible environment for your athletes, we'll explore what you can do in these six areas:

- Preseason physical examinations
- Physical conditioning
- Equipment and facilities inspection
- Matching athletes and inherent risks
- Proper supervision and record keeping
- Environmental conditions

We'll begin with what should take place before the season begins: the preseason physical examination.

Preseason Physical Examination

We recommend that your players have a physical examination before participating in hockey. The exam should address the most likely areas of medical concern and identify youngsters at high risk. We also suggest that you have players' parents or guardians sign a participation agreement form and a release form to allow their children to be treated in case of an emergency.

Physical Conditioning

Players need to be in, or get in, shape to play the game at the level expected. To do so, they'll need to have adequate cardiorespiratory fitness and muscular fitness.

Cardiorespiratory fitness involves the body's ability to store and use oxygen and fuels efficiently to power muscle contractions. As players get in better shape, their bodies are able to more efficiently deliver oxygen and fuels to muscles and carry off carbon dioxides and other wastes. Hockey involves lots of skating; most players will have to be able to be moving nearly continuously and making short bursts throughout a game.

An advantage of teaching hockey with the games approach is that kids are active during almost the entire practice; there is no standing around in lines, watching teammates take part in drills. Players will be attaining higher levels of cardiorespiratory fitness as the season progresses simply by taking part in practice. However, watch closely for signs of low levels of cardiorespiratory fitness; don't let your athletes do too much until they're fit. You might privately counsel youngsters who appear overly winded, suggesting that they train outside of practice to increase their fitness.

Muscular fitness encompasses strength, muscle endurance, power, speed, and flexibility. This type of fitness is affected by physical maturity, as well as strength training and other types of training. Your players will likely exhibit a relatively wide range of muscular fitness. Those who have greater muscular fitness will be able to skate faster and shoot harder. They will also sustain fewer muscular injuries, and any injuries that do occur will tend to be more minor in nature. And in case of injury, recovery rate is accelerated in those with higher levels of muscular fitness.

Two other components of fitness and injury prevention are the warm-up and the cool-down. Although young bodies are generally very limber, they, too, can get tight from inactivity. The warm-up should address each muscle group and get the heart rate elevated in preparation for strenuous activity. Have players warm up for 5 to 10 minutes by playing easy games and stretching.

As practice winds down, slow players' heart rates with an easy jog or walk. Then have players stretch for five minutes to help avoid stiff muscles and make them less tight before the next practice or contest.

Equipment and Facilities Inspection

Another way to prevent injuries is to check the quality and fit of all of the protective equipment used by your players. Inspect the equipment before you distribute it, after you have assigned the equipment, and regularly during the season. Ensure that all players have adequate equipment that meets minimum requirements and suggest that they wear any recommended optional equipment. Worn-out, damaged, lost, or outdated equipment must be replaced immediately.

Remember, also, to examine regularly the rink on which your players practice and play. Remove hazards, report conditions you cannot remedy, and request maintenance as necessary. If unsafe conditions exist, either make adaptations to avoid risk to your players' safety or stop the practice or game until safe conditions have been restored.

Player Match-Ups and Inherent Risks

We recommend you group teams in two-year age ranges if possible. You'll encounter fewer mismatches in physical maturation with narrow age ranges. Even so, two 12-year-old boys might differ by 90 pounds in weight, a foot in height, and three or four years in emotional and intellectual maturity. This presents dangers for the less mature. Whenever possible, match players against opponents of similar size and physical maturity. Such an approach gives smaller, less mature youngsters a better chance to succeed and avoid injury while providing more mature players with a greater challenge. Closely supervise games so that the more mature do not put the less mature at undue risk.

Proper matching helps protect you from certain liability concerns. But you must also warn players of the inherent risks involved in playing hockey, because "failure to warn" is one of the most successful arguments in lawsuits against coaches. So, thoroughly explain the inherent risks of hockey, and make sure each player knows, understands, and appreciates those risks.

The preseason parent-orientation meeting is a good opportunity to explain the risks of the sport to both parents and players. It is also a good occasion on which to have both the players and their parents sign waivers releasing you from liability should an injury occur. Such waivers do not relieve you of responsibility for your players' well-being, but they are recommended by lawyers.

Proper Supervision and Record Keeping

To ensure players' safety, you will need to provide both general supervision and specific supervision. General supervision is being in the area of activity so that you can see and hear what is happening. You should be

- immediately accessible to the activity and able to oversee the entire activity,
- alert to conditions that may be dangerous to players and ready to take action to protect them, and
- able to react immediately and appropriately to emergencies.

Specific supervision is direct supervision of an activity at practice. For example, you should provide specific supervision when you teach new skills and continue it until your athletes understand the requirements of the activity, the risks involved, and their own ability to perform in light of these risks. You need to also provide specific supervision when you notice either players breaking rules or a change in the condition of your athletes.

As a general rule, the more dangerous the activity, the more specific the supervision required. This suggests that more specific supervision is required with younger and less experienced athletes.

As part of your supervision duty, you are expected to foresee potentially dangerous situations and to be positioned to help prevent them from occurring. This requires that you know hockey well, especially the rules that are intended to provide for safety. Prohibit dangerous horseplay, and, if you play outdoors, hold practices only under safe weather conditions. These specific supervisory activities, applied consistently, will make the play environment safer for your players and will help protect you from liability if a mishap does occur.

For further protection, keep records of your season plans, practice plans, and players' injuries. Season and practice plans come in handy when you need evidence that players have been taught certain skills, whereas accurate, detailed injury-report forms offer protection against unfounded lawsuits. Ask for these forms from your sponsoring organization (appendix A has a sample injury report form), and hold onto these records for several years so that an "old hockey injury" of a former player doesn't come back to haunt you.

Environmental Conditions

Most problems due to environmental factors are related to excessive heat or cold, though you should also consider other environmental factors such as severe weather and pollution. Roller hockey players may be exposed to heat or cold, while ice hockey players may be exposed to cold. A little thought about the potential problems and a little effort to ensure adequate protection for your athletes will prevent most serious emergencies that are related to environmental conditions.

Heat

On hot, humid days the body has difficulty cooling itself. Because the air is already saturated with water vapor (humidity), sweat doesn't evaporate as easily. Therefore, body sweat is a less effective cooling agent, and the body retains extra heat. Hot, humid environments make athletes prone to heat exhaustion and heatstroke (see more on these in "Serious Injuries" on page 29). And if you think it's hot or humid, it's worse on the kids — not only because they're more active, but also because youngsters under the age of 12 have a more difficult time than adults regulating their body temperature. To provide for players' safety in hot or humid conditions, take the following preventive measures.

⊙ **Monitor weather conditions and adjust practices accordingly.** Figure 3.1 shows the specific air temperatures and humidity percentages that can be hazardous.

⊙ **Acclimatize players to exercising in high heat and humidity.** Athletes can make adjustments to high heat and humidity over 7 to 10 days. During this time, hold practices at low to moderate activity levels and give the players water breaks every 20 minutes.

⊙ **Switch to light clothing.** Players should wear shorts and white T-shirts.

⊙ **Identify and monitor players who are prone to heat illness.** Players who are overweight, heavily muscled, or out of shape will be more prone to heat illness, as are athletes who work excessively hard or who have suffered heat illness before. Closely monitor these athletes and give them water breaks every 15 to 20 minutes.

⊙ **Make sure athletes replace water lost through sweat.** Encourage your players to drink one liter of water each day outside of practice and contest times, to drink eight ounces of water every 20 minutes during practice or competition, and to drink four to eight ounces of water 20 minutes before practice or competition.

⊙ **Replenish electrolytes lost through sweat.** Sodium (salt) and potassium are lost through sweat. The best way to replace these nutrients is by eating a normal diet that contains fresh fruits and vegetables. Bananas are a good source of potassium. The normal American diet contains plenty of salt, so players don't need to go overboard in salting their food to replace lost sodium.

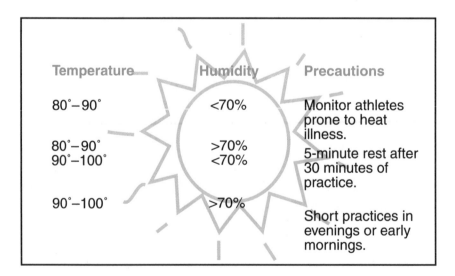

Temperature	Humidity	Precautions
80°–90°	<70%	Monitor athletes prone to heat illness.
80°–90° 90°–100°	>70% <70%	5-minute rest after 30 minutes of practice.
90°–100°	>70%	Short practices in evenings or early mornings.

Figure 3.1   Warm-environment conditions.

Water, Water Everywhere

Encourage players to drink plenty of water before, during, and after practice. Because water makes up 45 percent to 65 percent of a youngster's body weight and water weighs about a pound per pint, the loss of even a little bit of water can have severe consequences for the body's systems. And it doesn't have to be hot and humid for players to become dehydrated. Nor do players have to feel thirsty; in fact, by the time they are aware of their thirst, they are long overdue for a drink.

Cold

When a person is exposed to cold weather, the body temperature starts to drop below normal. To counteract this, the body shivers and reduces the blood flow to gain or conserve heat. But no matter how effective the body's natural heating mechanism is, the body will better withstand cold temperatures if it is prepared to handle them. To reduce the risk of cold-related illnesses, make sure players wear appropriate protective clothing, and keep them active to maintain body heat. Also monitor the windchill (see figure 3.2).

Severe Weather

Severe weather refers to a host of potential dangers, including lightning storms, tornadoes, hail, and heavy rains.

		Temperature (°F)								
		0	5	10	15	20	25	30	35	40
		Flesh may freeze within 1 minute								
	40	-55	-45	-35	-30	-20	-15	-5	0	10
	35	-50	-40	-35	-30	-20	-10	-5	5	10
Wind speed (mph)	30	-50	-40	-30	-25	-20	-10	0	5	10
	25	-45	-35	-30	-20	-15	-5	0	10	15
	20	-35	-30	-25	-15	-10	0	5	10	20
	15	-30	-25	-20	-10	-5	0	10	15	25
	10	-20	-15	-10	0	5	10	15	20	30
	5	-5	0	5	10	15	20	25	30	35

Windchill temperature (°F)

Figure 3.2   Windchill factor index.

Lightning is of special concern because it can come up quickly and can cause great harm or even kill. For each 5-second count from the flash of lightning to the bang of thunder, lightning is one mile away. A flash-bang of 10 seconds means lightning is two miles away; a flash-bang of 15 seconds indicates lightning is three miles away. A practice or competition should be stopped for the day if lightning is three miles away or less (15 seconds or less from flash to bang).

Safe places in which to take cover when lightning strikes are fully enclosed metal vehicles with the windows up, enclosed buildings, and low ground (under cover of bushes, if possible). It's not safe to be near metallic objects—flag poles, fences, light poles, metal bleachers, and so on. Also avoid trees, water, and open fields.

Cancel practice when under either a tornado watch or warning. If for some reason you are practicing or competing when a tornado is nearby, you should get inside a building if possible. If not, lie in a ditch or other low-lying area or crouch near a strong building, and use your arms to protect your head and neck.

The keys to handling severe weather are caution and prudence. Don't try to get that last 10 minutes of practice in if lightning is on the horizon. Don't continue to play in heavy rains. Many storms can strike both quickly and ferociously. Respect the weather and play it safe.

Air Pollution

Poor air quality and smog can present real dangers to your players, even playing indoors. Both short- and long-term lung damage are possible from participating in unsafe air. While it's true that participating in clean air is not possible in many areas, restricting activity is recommended when the air-quality ratings are worse than moderate or when there is a smog alert. Your local health department or air-quality control board can inform you of the air-quality ratings for your area and when restricting activities is recommended.

Responding to Players' Injuries

No matter how good and thorough your prevention program is, injuries may occur. When injury does strike, chances are you will be the one in charge. The severity and nature of the injury will determine how actively involved you'll be in treating the injury. But regardless of how seriously a player is hurt, it is your responsibility to know what steps to take. So let's look at how you should prepare to provide basic emergency care to your injured athletes and take the appropriate action when an injury does occur.

Being Prepared

Being prepared to provide basic emergency care involves three steps: being trained in cardiopulmonary resuscitation (CPR) and first aid, having an appropriately stocked first-aid kit on hand at practices and games, and having an emergency plan.

CPR and First-Aid Training

We recommend that all coaches receive CPR and first-aid training from a nationally recognized organization (the National Safety Council, the American Heart Association, the American Red Cross, or the American Sport Education Program). You should be certified based on a practical test and a written test of knowledge. CPR training should include pediatric and adult basic life support and obstructed airway procedures.

First-Aid Kit

A well-stocked first-aid kit should include the following:

- List of emergency phone numbers
- Change for a pay phone
- Face shield (for rescue breathing and CPR)
- Bandage scissors
- Plastic bags for crushed ice
- 3-inch and 4-inch elastic wraps
- Triangular bandages
- Sterile gauze pads—3-inch and 4-inch squares
- Saline solution for eyes
- Contact lens case
- Mirror
- Penlight
- Tongue depressors
- Cotton swabs
- Butterfly strips
- Bandage strips—assorted sizes
- Alcohol or peroxide
- Antibacterial soap
- First-aid cream or antibacterial ointment
- Petroleum jelly

- Tape adherent and tape remover
- 1 1/2-inch white athletic tape
- Prewrap
- Sterile gauze rolls
- Insect sting kit
- Safety pins
- 1/8-inch, 1/4-inch, and 1/2-inch foam rubber
- Disposable surgical gloves
- Thermometer

Emergency Plan

An emergency plan is the final step in preparing to take appropriate action for severe or serious injuries. The plan calls for three steps:

1. **Evaluate the injured player.** Your CPR and first aid training will guide you here.

2. **Call the appropriate medical personnel.** If possible, delegate the responsibility of seeking medical help to another calm and responsible adult who is on hand for all practices and games. Write out a list of emergency phone numbers and keep it with you at practices and games. Include the following phone numbers:

- Rescue unit
- Hospital
- Physician
- Police
- Fire department

Take each athlete's emergency information to every practice and game (see appendix B). This information includes the person to contact in case of an emergency, what types of medications the athlete is using, what types of drugs he or she is allergic to, and so on.

Give an emergency response card (see appendix C) to the contact person calling for emergency assistance. This provides the information the contact person needs to convey and will help keep the person calm, knowing that everything he or she needs to communicate is on the card. Also complete an injury report form (see appendix A) and keep it on file for any injury that occurs.

3. **Provide first aid.** If medical personnel are not on hand at the time of the injury, you should provide first aid care to the extent of your

qualifications. Again, while your CPR and first aid training will guide you here, the following are important guidelines:

- Do not move the injured athlete if the injury is to the head, neck, or back; if a large joint (ankle, knee, elbow, shoulder) is dislocated; or if the pelvis, a rib, or an arm or leg is fractured.
- Calm the injured athlete and keep others away from him or her as much as possible.
- Evaluate whether the athlete's breathing is stopped or irregular, and if necessary, clear the airway with your fingers.
- Administer artificial respiration if the athlete's breathing has stopped. Administer CPR if the athlete's circulation has stopped.
- Remain with the athlete until medical personnel arrive.

Emergency Steps

Your emergency plan should follow this sequence:

1. Check the athlete's level of consciousness.
2. Send a contact person to call the appropriate medical personnel and to call the athlete's parents.
3. Send someone to wait for the rescue team and direct them to the injured athlete.
4. Assess the injury.
5. Administer first aid.
6. Assist emergency medical personnel in preparing the athlete for transportation to a medical facility.
7. Appoint someone to go with the athlete if the parents are not available. This person should be responsible, calm, and familiar with the athlete. Assistant coaches or parents are best for this job.
8. Complete an injury report form while the incident is fresh in your mind (see appendix A).

Taking Appropriate Action

Proper CPR and first aid training, a well-stocked first aid kit, and an emergency plan help prepare you to take appropriate action when an injury occurs. We spoke in the previous section about the importance of providing first aid to the extent of your qualifications. Don't "play doctor" with injuries; sort out minor injuries that you can treat from those for which you need to call for medical assistance.

Next we'll look at taking the appropriate action for minor injuries and more serious injuries.

Minor Injuries

Although no injury seems minor to the person experiencing it, most injuries are neither life-threatening nor severe enough to restrict participation. When such injuries occur, you can take an active role in their initial treatment.

Scrapes and Cuts. When one of your players has an open wound, the first thing you should do is put on a pair of disposable surgical gloves or some other effective blood barrier. Then follow these four steps:

1. *Stop the bleeding* by applying direct pressure with a clean dressing to the wound and elevating it. The player may be able to apply this pressure while you put on your gloves. Do not remove the dressing if it becomes soaked with blood. Instead, place an additional dressing on top of the one already in place. If bleeding continues, elevate the injured area above the heart and maintain pressure.

2. *Cleanse the wound* thoroughly once the bleeding is controlled. A good rinsing with a forceful stream of water, and perhaps light scrubbing with soap, will help prevent infection.

3. *Protect the wound* with sterile gauze or a bandage strip. If the player continues to participate, apply protective padding over the injured area.

4. *Remove and dispose of gloves* carefully to prevent you or anyone else from coming into contact with blood.

For bloody noses not associated with serious facial injury, have the athlete sit and lean slightly forward. Then pinch the player's nostrils shut. If the bleeding continues after several minutes, or if the athlete has a history of nosebleeds, seek medical assistance.

Treating Bloody Injuries

You shouldn't let a fear of acquired immune deficiency syndrome (AIDS) stop you from helping a player. You are only at risk if you allow contaminated blood to come in contact with an open wound, so the surgical disposable gloves that you wear will protect you from AIDS should one of your players carry this disease. Check with your director or your organization for more information about protecting yourself and your participants from AIDS.

Strains and Sprains. The physical demands of hockey practices and games often result in injury to the muscles or tendons (strains) or to the ligaments (sprains). When your players suffer minor strains or sprains, immediately apply the PRICE method of injury care:

P – Protect the athlete and injured body part from further danger or trauma.

R – Rest the area to avoid further damage and foster healing.

I – Ice the area to reduce swelling and pain.

C – Compress the area by securing an ice bag in place with an elastic wrap.

E – Elevate the injury above heart level to keep the blood from pooling in the area.

Bumps and Bruises. Inevitably, hockey players make contact with each other and with the rink. If the force applied to a body part at impact is great enough, a bump or bruise will result. Many players continue playing with such sore spots, but if the bump or bruise is large and painful, you should act appropriately. Use the PRICE method for injury care and monitor the injury. If swelling, discoloration, and pain have lessened, the player may resume participation with protective padding; if not, the player should be examined by a physician.

Serious Injuries

Head, neck, and back injuries; fractures; and injuries that cause a player to lose consciousness are among a class of injuries that you cannot and should not try to treat yourself. In these cases you should follow the emergency plan outlined on page 27. We do want to examine more closely your role, however, in preventing and handling two heat illnesses: heat exhaustion and heatstroke.

Heat Exhaustion. Heat exhaustion is a shocklike condition caused by dehydration and electrolyte depletion. Symptoms include headache, nausea, dizziness, chills, fatigue, and extreme thirst. Profuse sweating is a key sign of heat exhaustion. Other signs include pale, cool, and clammy skin; rapid, weak pulse; loss of coordination; and dilated pupils. See figure 3.3 for signs and symptoms of heat exhaustion.

A player suffering from heat exhaustion should rest in a cool, shaded area; drink cool water; and have ice applied to the neck, back, or abdomen to help cool the body. You may have to administer CPR if necessary or send for emergency medical assistance if the athlete doesn't recover or his or her condition worsens. Under no conditions should the athlete return to activity that day or before he or she regains all the weight lost through sweat. If the player had to see a physician, he or she shouldn't return to the team until he or she has a written release from the physician.

Heatstroke. Heatstroke is a life-threatening condition in which the body stops sweating and body temperature rises dangerously high. It occurs when dehydration causes a malfunction in the body's temperature control center in the brain. Symptoms include the feeling of being on fire (extremely hot), nausea, confusion, irritability, and fatigue. Signs include hot, dry, and flushed or red skin (this is a key sign); lack of sweat; rapid pulse; rapid breathing; constricted pupils; vomiting; diarrhea; and possibly seizures, unconsciousness, or respiratory or cardiac arrest. See figure 3.3 for signs and symptoms of heatstroke.

Send for emergency medical assistance immediately and have the player rest in a cool, shaded area. Remove excess clothing and equipment from the player, and cool the player's body with cool, wet towels

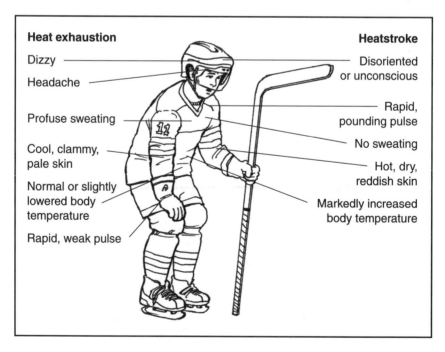

Figure 3.3   Signs and symptoms of heat exhaustion and heatstroke.

or by pouring cool water over him or her. Apply ice packs to the arm-pits, neck, back, abdomen, and between the legs. If the player is conscious, have him or her drink cool water. If the player is unconscious, place the player on his or her side to allow fluids and vomit to drain from the mouth.

An athlete who has suffered heatstroke may not return to the team until he or she has a written release from a physician.

Protecting Yourself

When one of your players is injured, naturally your first concern is his or her well-being. Your feelings for youngsters, after all, are what made you decide to coach. Unfortunately, there is something else that you must consider: Can you be held liable for the injury?

From a legal standpoint, a coach has nine duties to fulfill. We've discussed all but planning in this chapter. The following is a summary of your legal duties:

1. Provide a safe environment.
2. Properly plan the activity.
3. Provide adequate and proper equipment.
4. Match, or equate, athletes.
5. Warn of inherent risks in the sport.
6. Supervise the activity closely.
7. Evaluate athletes for injury or incapacitation.
8. Know emergency procedures and first aid.
9. Keep adequate records.

Keep records of your season plan and practice plans and of players' injuries. Season and practice plans come in handy when you need evidence that players have been taught certain skills, and injury reports offer protection against unfounded lawsuits. Hold onto these records for several years so that an "old injury" of a former player doesn't come back to haunt you.

In addition to fulfilling these nine legal duties, you should check your organization's insurance coverage and your insurance coverage to make sure these policies will protect you from liability.

The Games Approach to Coaching Hockey

Do you remember how as a kid you were taught by adults to play a sport, either in an organized sport program or physical education class? They probably taught you the basic skills using a series of drills that, if the truth be known, you found very boring. As you began to learn the basic skills, they eventually taught you the tactics of the game, showing you when to use these skills in various game situations. Do you remember how impatient you became during what seemed to be endless instruction, and how much you just wanted to play? Well, forget this traditional approach to teaching sports.

Now can you recall learning a sport by playing with a group of your friends in the neighborhood? You didn't learn the basic skills first; no time for that. You began playing immediately. If you didn't know the basic things to do, your friends told you quickly during the game so they could keep playing. Try to remember, because we're going to ask you to use a very similar approach to teaching hockey to young people called the games approach, an approach we think knocks the socks off the traditional approach.

On the surface, it would seem to make sense to introduce hockey by first teaching the basic skills of the sport and then the tactics of the game, but we've discovered that this approach has disadvantages. First, it teaches the skills of the sport out of the context of the game. Kids may learn to use their backhand and to pass the puck, but they find it difficult to use these skills in the real game. This is because they do not yet understand the fundamental tactics of hockey and do not appreciate how best to use their newfound skills.

Second, learning skills by doing drills outside of the context of the game is so-o-o-o boring. The single biggest turnoff about adults teaching kids sports is that we overorganize the instruction and deprive kids of their intrinsic desire to play the game.

As a coach we're asking that you teach hockey the games approach way. Clear the traditional approach out of your mind. Once you fully understand the games approach, you'll quickly see its superiority in teaching hockey. Not only will kids learn the game better, but you and your players will have much more fun. And as a bonus, you'll have far fewer discipline problems.

With the games approach to teaching hockey, we begin with a game. This will be a modified and much smaller game designed to suit the age and ability of the players. As the kids play in these "mini" games, you can begin to help them understand the nature of the game and to appreciate simple concepts of positioning and tactics. When your players understand what they must do in the game, they are then eager to develop the skills to play the game. Now that players are motivated to learn the skills, you can demonstrate the skills of the game, practice using game-like drills, and provide individual instruction by identifying players' errors and helping to correct them.

In the traditional approach to teaching sports, players do this:

Learn the skill → **Learn the tactics** → **Play the game**

In the games approach players do this:

Play the game → **Learn the tactics** → **Learn the skill**

In the past we have placed too much emphasis on the learning of skills and not enough on learning how to play skillfully—that is, how to use those skills in competition. The games approach, in contrast, emphasizes learning what to do first, then how to do it. Moreover— and this is a really important point—the games approach lets kids discover what to do in the game not by you telling them, but by their experiencing it. What you do as an effective coach is help them discover what they've experienced.

In contrast to the "skill-drill-kill the enthusiasm" approach, the games approach is a guided discovery method of teaching. It empowers your kids to solve the problems that arise in the game, and that's a big part of the fun in learning a game.

Now let's look more closely at the games approach to see the four-step process for teaching hockey:

1. Play a modified hockey game.
2. Help the players discover what they need to do to play the game successfully.
3. Teach the skills of the game.
4. Practice the skills in another game.

Step 1. Play a Modified Hockey Game

Okay, it's the first day of practice; some of the kids are eager to get started, while others are obviously apprehensive. Some have rarely skated, most don't know the rules, and none knows the positions in hockey. What do you do?

If you use the traditional approach, you start with a little warm-up activity, then line the players up for a simple passing drill and go from there. With the games approach, you begin by playing a modified game that is developmentally appropriate for the level of the players and also designed to focus on learning a specific part of the game.

Modifying the game emphasizes a limited number of situations in the game. This is one way you "guide" your players to discover certain tactics in the game.

For instance, you have your players play a 3 v 3 (three players versus three players) cross-ice game. The objective of the game is to make three passes before attempting to score. Playing the game this way forces players to think about what they have to do to keep possession of the puck.

Step 2. Help the Players Discover What They Need to Do

As your players are playing the game, look for the right spot to "freeze" the action, step in, and hold a brief question-and-answer session to discuss problems they were having in carrying out the goals of the game. You don't need to pop in on the first miscue, but if they repeat the same types of mental or physical mistakes a few times in a row, step in and ask them questions that relate to the aim of the game and the necessary skills required. The best time to interrupt the game is when you notice that they are having trouble carrying out the main goal, or aim, of the game. By stopping the game, freezing action, and asking questions, you'll help them understand

- what the aim of the game is,
- what they must do to achieve that aim, and
- what skills they must use to achieve that aim.

For example, if your players are playing a game in which the objective is one-touch passing, but they are having trouble doing so, interrupt the action and ask the following questions:

Coach: What are you supposed to do in this game?

Players: Pass the puck four times before scoring.

Coach: What does your team have to do to keep the puck for four passes in a row?

Players: Pass the puck.

Coach: Yes, and what else?

Players: You have to be able to get the pass, too.

Coach: OK. You have to be able to pass the puck and get the puck when it's passed. Why don't we practice passing the puck and receiving the pass?

Through the modified game and skillful questioning on your part, your players realize that stick control skills are essential to their success in one-touch passing. Just as important, rather than telling them that stick control skills are critical, you led them to that discovery through a well-designed modified game and through questions. This questioning that leads to players' discovery is a crucial part of the games approach. Essentially you'll be asking your players—usually literally—"What do you need to do to succeed in this situation?"

Asking the right questions is a very important part of your teaching. At first asking questions will be difficult because your players have little or no experience with the game. And if you've learned sport through the traditional approach, you'll be tempted to tell your players how to play the game and not waste time asking them questions. Resist this powerful temptation to tell them what to do, and especially don't do so before they begin to play the game.

If your players have trouble understanding what to do, phrase your questions to let them choose between one option versus another. For example, if you ask them "What's the fastest way to get the puck down the ice?" and get answers such as "Hit it," then ask, "Is it passing or carrying the puck?"

Immediately following the question-and-answer session you will begin a skill practice, which is Step 3 of the four-step process.

Sometimes players simply need to have more time playing the game, or you may need to modify the game further so that it is even easier for them to discover what they are to do. It'll take more patience on your part, but it's a powerful way to learn. Don't be reluctant to change the numbers in the teams or some aspect of the structure of the game to aid this discovery. In fact, we advocate playing "odd-player" games (e.g., 3 v 1, 3 v 2) in the second game of each practice; we'll explain this concept in a moment.

Step 3. Teach the Skills of the Game

Only when your players recognize the skills they need to be successful in the game do you want to teach the specific skills through focused drills. This is when you use a more traditional approach to teaching sport skills, the "IDEA" approach, which we will describe in chapter 5.

Step 4. Practice the Skills in Another Game

Once the players have practiced the skill, you then put them in another game situation—this time an odd-player game (e.g., 3 v 1, 3 v 2). Why use team pairings of odd and even numbers of players? It's simple: As a coach, you want your players to experience success as they're learning skills. The best way to experience success early on is to create an advantage for the players. This makes it more likely that, for instance, in a 3 v 1 game, your three offensive players will be able to make four passes before attempting to score.

A good way to practice is to use even-sided games (e.g., 3 v 3, 6 v 6) in Game 1s and odd-player games in Game 2s. The reasoning behind this is to introduce players to a situation similar to what they will experience in competition, and to let them discover the challenges they face in performing the necessary skill. Then you teach them the skill, have them practice it, and put them back in another game—this time an odd-player game to give them a greater chance of experiencing success.

As players improve their skills you don't need to use odd-player games. At a certain point having a 3 v 1 or 6 v 3 advantage will be too easy for the kids and won't challenge them to hone their skills. At that point you lessen the advantage to, say, 3 v 2 or 6 v 4, or you may even decide that they're ready to practice the skill in even-sided competition. The key is to set up situations where your athletes experience success, yet are challenged in doing so. This will take careful monitoring on your part, but having kids play odd-player games as they are learning skills is a very effective way of helping them learn and improve.

And that's the games approach. Your players will get to play more in practice, and once they learn how the skills fit into their performance and enjoyment of the game, they'll be more motivated to work on those skills, which will help them to be successful.

Teaching and Shaping Skills

Coaching hockey is about teaching tactics, skills, fitness, values, and other useful things. It's also about "coaching" players before, during, and after contests. Teaching and coaching are closely related, but there are important differences. In this chapter we'll focus on principles of teaching, especially on teaching hockey skills. But many of the principles we'll discuss apply to teaching tactics, fitness concepts, and values as well. (Most of the other important teaching principles deal with communication, covered in chapter 2.) Then in chapter 6 we'll discuss the principles of coaching, which refer to your leadership activities during contests.

Teaching Hockey Skills

Many people believe that the only qualification needed to teach a skill is to have performed it. It's helpful to have performed it, but there is much more than that to teaching successfully. And even if you haven't performed the skill before, you can still learn to teach successfully with the useful acronym IDEA:

I – Introduce the skill.

D – Demonstrate the skill.

E – Explain the skill.

A – Attend to players practicing the skill.

These are the basic steps of good teaching. Now we'll explain each step in greater detail.

Introduce the Skill

Players, especially young and inexperienced ones, need to know what skill they are learning and why they are learning it. You should therefore take these three steps every time you introduce a skill to your players:

1. Get your players' attention.
2. Name the skill.
3. Explain the importance of the skill.

Get Your Players' Attention

Because youngsters are easily distracted, use some method to get their attention. Some coaches use interesting news items or stories. Others use jokes. And still others simply project enthusiasm to get their players to listen. Whatever method you use, speak slightly above the normal volume and look your players in the eye when you speak.

Also, position players so they can see and hear you. Arrange the players in two or three evenly spaced rows, facing you. (Make sure they aren't looking into the sun or at some distracting activity.) Then ask if all of them can see you before you begin.

Name the Skill

Although you might mention other common names for the skill, decide which one you'll use and stick with it. This will help avoid confusion and enhance communication among your players.

Explain the Importance of the Skill

Although the importance of a skill may be apparent to you, your players may be less able to see how the skill will help them become better hockey players. Offer them a reason for learning the skill and describe how the skill relates to more advanced skills.

> *The most difficult aspect of coaching is this: Coaches must learn to let athletes learn. Sport skills should be taught so they have meaning to the child, not just meaning to the coach.*
>
> — Rainer Martens, founder of the American Sport Education Program

Demonstrate the Skill

The demonstration step is the most important part of teaching sport skills to players who may never have done anything closely resembling the skill. They need a picture, not just words. They need to see how the skill is performed.

If you are unable to perform the skill correctly, have an assistant coach, one of your players, or someone else more skilled perform the demonstration. These tips will help make your demonstrations more effective:

⊙ Use correct form.

⊙ Demonstrate the skill several times.

⊙ Slow down the action, if possible, during one or two performances so players can see every movement involved in the skill.

⊙ Perform the skill at different angles so your players can get a full perspective of it.

⊙ Demonstrate the skill with both the right and the left legs or the right and the left arms.

Explain the Skill

Players learn more effectively when they're given a brief explanation of the skill along with the demonstration. Use simple terms and, if possible, relate the skill to previously learned skills. Ask your players whether they understand your description. A good technique is to ask the team to repeat your explanation. Ask questions like "What are you going to do first?" and "Then what?" Watch for when players look confused or uncertain, and repeat your explanation and demonstration at those points. If possible, use different words so your players get a chance to try to understand the skill from a different perspective.

Complex skills often are better understood when they are explained in more manageable parts. For instance, if you want to teach your players how to skate backward, you might take the following steps:

1. Show them a correct performance of the entire skill, and explain its function in hockey.

2. Break down the skill and point out its component parts to your players.

3. Have players perform each of the component skills you have already taught them, such as bending their knees, sitting down as if they were in a chair, beginning to skate by making a C with one skate blade, thrusting the leg completely out from the body, bringing the leg back quickly underneath the body, and preparing the other leg to thrust into a C cut.

4. After players have demonstrated their ability to perform the separate parts of the skill in sequence, reexplain the entire skill.

5. Have players practice the skill in gamelike conditions.

One caution: Young players have short attention spans, and a long demonstration or explanation of the skill will bore them. So spend no more than a few minutes altogether on the introduction, demonstration, and explanation phases. Then get the players active in a game that calls on them to perform the skill. The total IDEA should be completed in 10 minutes or less, followed by games in which players practice the skill.

Attend to Players Practicing the Skill

If the skill you selected was within your players' capabilities and you have done an effective job of introducing, demonstrating, and explaining it, your players should be ready to attempt the skill. Some players may need to be physically guided through the movements during their first few attempts. Walking unsure athletes through the skill in this way will help them gain confidence to perform the skill on their own.

Your teaching duties don't end when all your athletes have demonstrated that they understand how to perform the skill. In fact, a significant part of your teaching will involve observing closely the hit-and-miss trial performances of your players. In the next section we'll guide you in shaping players' skills, and then we'll help you learn how to detect and correct errors, using positive feedback. Keep in mind that your feedback will have a great influence on your players' motivation to practice and improve their performances.

Remember, too, that players need individual instruction. So set aside a time before, during, or after practice to give individual help.

Helping Players Improve Skills

After you have successfully taught your players the fundamentals of a skill, your focus will be on helping them improve that skill. Players will learn skills and improve upon them at different rates, so don't get too frustrated. Instead, help them improve by shaping their skills and detecting and correcting errors.

Shaping Players' Skills

One of your principal teaching duties is to reward positive behavior—in terms of successful skill execution—when you see it. A player makes a good pass in practice, and you immediately say, "That's the way to drive through it! Good follow through!" This, plus a smile and a "thumbs-up" gesture, go a long way toward reinforcing that technique in that player. However, sometimes you may have a long, dry spell before you have any correct technique to reinforce. It's difficult to reward players when they aren't executing skills correctly. How can you shape their skills if this is the case?

Shaping skills takes practice on your players' part and patience on your part. Expect your players to make errors. Telling the player who made the great pass that she did a good job doesn't ensure that she'll make that pass the next time. Seeing inconsistency in your players' techniques can be frustrating. It's even more challenging to stay positive when your athletes repeatedly perform a skill incorrectly or lack enthusiasm for learning. It can certainly be frustrating to see athletes who seemingly don't heed your advice and continue to make the same mistakes. And when the athletes don't seem to care, you may wonder why you should.

Please know that it is normal to get frustrated at times when teaching skills. Nevertheless, part of successful coaching is controlling this frustration. Instead of getting upset, use these six guidelines for shaping skills:

1. Think small initially. Reward the first signs of behavior that approximate what you want. Then reward closer and closer approximations of the desired behavior. In short, use your reward power to shape the behavior you seek.

2. Break skills into small steps. For instance, in learning to handle the puck, one of your players does well in watching for defenders around the puck, but he's careless with the puck and doesn't effectively shield the puck from defenders. He often has the puck too far away from him as he carries it, or he skates too fast and loses control of the puck. Reinforce the correct technique of watching for defenders, and teach him how to keep the puck at stick's length. When he masters that, focus on getting him to skate at a speed at which he can control the puck.

3. Develop one component of a skill at a time. Don't try to shape two components of a skill at once. For example, in executing a shot off of a pass, players must control the puck first and then shoot it at the net. Players should focus first on one aspect (stopping the puck by cushioning, the hands giving with the puck), then on the other (dragging the puck forward for the shot). Athletes who have problems mastering a skill often do so because they're trying to improve two or more components at once. Help these athletes to isolate a single component.

4. As athletes become more proficient at a skill, reinforce them only occasionally and only for the best examples of the skill behavior. By focusing only on the best examples, you will help them continue to improve once they've mastered the basics.

5. When athletes are trying to master a new skill, temporarily relax your standards for how you reward them. As they focus on the new skill or attempt to integrate it with other skills, the old, well-learned skills may temporarily degenerate.

6. If, however, a well-learned skill degenerates for long, you may need to restore it by going back to the basics.

Coaches often have more skilled players provide feedback to teammates as they practice skills. This can be effective, but proceed with caution: You must tell the skilled players exactly what to look for when their teammates are performing the skills. You must also tell them the corrections for the common errors of that skill.

We've looked at how to guide your athletes as they learn skills. Now let's look at another critical teaching principle that you should employ as you're shaping skills: detecting and correcting errors.

Detecting and Correcting Errors

Good coaches recognize that athletes make two types of errors: learning errors and performance errors. Learning errors are ones that occur because athletes don't know how to perform a skill; that is, they have not yet developed the correct motor program in the brain to perform a particular skill. Performance errors are made not because athletes don't know how to do the skill, but because they made a mistake in executing what they do know. There is no easy way to know whether a player is making learning or performance errors. Part of the art of coaching is being able to sort out which type of error each mistake is.

The process of helping your athletes correct errors begins with your observing and evaluating their performances to determine if the mistakes are learning or performance errors. For performance errors, you need to look for the reasons that your athletes are not performing as well as they know how. If the mistakes are learning errors, then you need to help them learn the skill, which is the focus of this section.

There is no substitute for knowing skills well in correcting learning errors. The better you understand a skill—not only how it is done correctly but also what causes learning errors—the more helpful you will be in correcting mistakes.

One of the most common coaching mistakes is to provide inaccurate feedback and advice on how to correct errors. Don't rush into error correction; wrong feedback or poor advice will hurt the learning process more than no feedback or advice. If you are uncertain about the cause of the problem or how to correct it, continue to observe and analyze until you are more sure. As a rule, you should see the error repeated several times before attempting to correct it.

Correct One Error at a Time

Suppose Jill, one of your forwards, is having trouble with her shooting. She's doing most things well, but you notice that she's not pointing her stick at the net on her follow-through, and she often shoots the puck from the end of the stick blade or "the toe." This does not allow her to control the puck through the shooting motion and generate good power and accuracy. What do you do?

First, decide which error to correct first, because athletes learn more effectively when they attempt to correct one error at a time. Determine whether one error is causing the other; if so, have the athlete correct that error first, because it may eliminate the other error. In Jill's case, however, neither error is causing the other. In such cases, athletes should correct the error that will bring the greatest improvement when remedied—for Jill, this probably is shooting the puck from the toe of the stick. Improvement here will likely motivate her to correct the other error.

Use Positive Feedback to Correct Errors

The positive approach to correcting errors includes emphasizing what to do instead of what not to do. Use compliments, praise, rewards, and encouragement to correct errors. Acknowledge correct performance as well as efforts to improve. By using the positive approach, you can help your athletes feel good about themselves and promote a strong desire to achieve.

When you're working with one athlete at a time, the positive approach to correcting errors includes four steps:

1. Praise effort and correct performance.
2. Give simple and precise feedback to correct errors.
3. Make sure the athlete understands your feedback.
4. Provide an environment that motivates the athlete to improve.

Let's take a brief look at each step.

Step 1: Praise Effort and Correct Performance. Praise your athlete for trying to perform a skill correctly and for performing any parts of it correctly. Praise the athlete immediately after he or she performs the skill, if possible. Keep the praise simple: "Good try," "Way to hustle," or "Good form," "Good extension," "That's the way to follow through." You can also use nonverbal feedback, such as smiling, clapping your hands, or any facial or body expression that shows approval.

Make sure you're sincere with your praise. Don't indicate that an athlete's effort was good when it wasn't. Usually an athlete knows when he or she has made a sincere effort to perform the skill correctly and perceives undeserved praise for what it is—untruthful feedback to make him or her feel good. Likewise, don't indicate that a player's performance was correct when it wasn't.

Step 2: Give Simple and Precise Feedback. Don't burden a player with a long or detailed explanation of how to correct an error. Give just enough feedback so the player can correct one error at a time. Before giving feedback, recognize that some athletes will readily accept it immediately after the error; others will respond better if you slightly delay the correction.

For errors that are complicated to explain and difficult to correct, try the following:

- Explain and demonstrate what the athlete should have done. Do not demonstrate what the athlete did wrong.
- Explain the cause or causes of the error, if this isn't obvious.
- Explain why you are recommending the correction you have selected, if it's not obvious.

Step 3: Make Sure the Athlete Understands Your Feedback. If the athlete doesn't understand your feedback, he or she won't be able to correct the error. Ask him or her to repeat the feedback and to explain and demonstrate how it will be used. If the athlete can't do this, be patient and present your feedback again. Then have the athlete repeat the feedback after you're finished.

Step 4: Provide an Environment That Motivates the Athlete to Improve. Your players won't always be able to correct their errors immediately even if they do understand your feedback. Encourage them to "hang tough" and stick with it when corrections are difficult or they seem discouraged. For more difficult corrections, remind them that it will take time, and the improvement will happen only if they work at it. Look to encourage players with low self-confidence. Saying something like, "You handled the puck at a much better speed today; with practice, you'll be able to keep the puck out away from your body so you can pass, make a move, or shoot," can motivate a player to continue to refine his or her dribbling skills.

Some athletes need to be more motivated to improve. Others may be very self-motivated and need little help from you in this area at all; with them you can practically ignore Step 4 when correcting an error. While motivation comes from within, look to provide an environment of positive instruction and encouragement to help your athletes improve.

A final note on correcting errors: Team sports such as hockey provide unique challenges in this endeavor. How do you provide individual feedback in a group setting using a positive approach? Instead of yelling across the rink to correct an error (and embarrassing the player), substitute for the player who erred. Then make the correction on the sidelines. This type of feedback has three advantages:

- The player will be more receptive to the one-on-one feedback.
- The other players are still active, still practicing skills, and unable to hear your discussion.
- Because the rest of the team is still playing, you'll feel compelled to make your comments simple and concise—which, as we've said, is more helpful to the player.

This doesn't mean you can't use the team setting to give specific, positive feedback. You can do so to emphasize correct group and individual performances. Use this team feedback approach only for positive statements, though. Keep any negative feedback for individual discussions.

Developing Practice Plans

You will need to create practice plans for each season. Each practice plan should contain the following sections:

- Purpose
- Equipment
- Plan

Purpose sections focus on what you want to teach your players during each practice; they outline your main theme for each practice. The purpose should be drawn from your season plan (see chapter 9). Equipment sections note what you'll need to have on hand for that practice. Plan sections outline what you will do during each practice session. Each consists of these elements:

- Warm-Up
- Game
- Skill Development
- Game
- Cool-Down and Review

You'll begin each session with about five minutes of warm-up activities. Then you'll have your players play a modified hockey game (look in chapter 8 for suggested games). You'll look for your cue to interrupt that game—your cue being when players are having problems with carrying out the basic goal or aim of the game. At this point you'll "freeze" the action, keeping the players where they are, and ask brief questions about the tactical problems the players encountered and what skills they need to solve those problems. (Review chapter 4 for more on interrupting a game and holding a question-and-answer session.)

Then you'll teach the skill the players need to acquire to successfully execute the tactic. During Skill Practice you'll use the IDEA approach:

- Introduce the skill.
- Demonstrate the skill.

⊙ Explain the skill.

⊙ Attend to players practicing the skill.

Your introduction, demonstration, and explanation of a skill should take no more than two to three minutes; then you'll attend to players and provide teaching cues or further demonstration as necessary as they practice the skill.

After the Skill Practices, you will usually have the athletes play another game or two to let them use the skills they have just learned and to understand them in the context of a game. During Game and Skill Practices, emphasize the importance of every player on the court moving and being involved in every play, whether they will be directly touching the ball or backing up their teammates. No player should be standing around.

The Plan section continues with a cool-down and stretch. Following this you'll wrap up the practice with a few summary comments and remind them of the next practice or game day.

The games in chapter 8 include suggestions to help you modify the games. These suggestions will help you keep practices fun and provide activities for players with varying skill levels.

Although practicing using the games approach should reduce the need for discipline, there will be times when you'll have to deal with players who are misbehaving in practice. In the next section we'll help you handle these situations.

Dealing With Misbehavior

Athletes will misbehave at times; it's only natural. Following are two ways you can respond to misbehavior: through extinction or discipline.

Extinction

Ignoring a misbehavior—neither rewarding nor disciplining it—is called extinction. This can be effective under certain circumstances. In some situations, disciplining young people's misbehavior only encourages them to act up further because of the recognition they get. Ignoring misbehavior teaches youngsters that it is not worth your attention.

Sometimes, though, you cannot wait for a behavior to fizzle out. When players cause danger to themselves or others or disrupt the activities of others, you need to take immediate action. Tell the offending player that the behavior must stop and that discipline will follow if it doesn't. If the athlete doesn't stop misbehaving after the warning, discipline.

Extinction also doesn't work well when a misbehavior is self-rewarding. For example, you may be able to keep from grimacing if a youngster kicks you in the shin, but he or she still knows you were hurt. Therein lies the reward. In these circumstances, it is also necessary to discipline the player for the undesirable behavior.

Extinction works best in situations in which players are seeking recognition through mischievous behaviors, clowning, or grandstanding. Usually, if you are patient, their failure to get your attention will cause the behavior to disappear.

However, be alert that you don't extinguish desirable behavior. When youngsters do something well, they expect to be positively reinforced. Not rewarding them will likely cause them to discontinue the desired behavior.

Discipline

Some educators say we should never discipline young people, but should only reinforce their positive behaviors. They argue that discipline does not work, creates hostility, and sometimes develops avoidance behaviors that may be more unwholesome than the original problem behavior. It is true that discipline does not always work and that it can create problems when used ineffectively, but when used appropriately, discipline is effective in eliminating undesirable behaviors without creating other undesirable consequences. You must use discipline effectively, because it is impossible to guide athletes through positive reinforcement and extinction alone. Discipline is part of the positive approach when these guidelines are followed:

⊙ Discipline in a corrective way to help athletes improve now and in the future. Don't discipline to retaliate and make yourself feel better.

⊙ Impose discipline in an impersonal way when athletes break team rules or otherwise misbehave. Shouting at or scolding athletes indicates that your attitude is one of revenge.

⊙ Once a good rule has been agreed upon, ensure that athletes who violate it experience the unpleasant consequences of their misbehavior. Don't wave discipline threateningly over their heads. Just do it, but warn an athlete once before disciplining.

⊙ Be consistent in administering discipline.

⊙ Don't discipline using consequences that may cause you guilt. If you can't think of an appropriate consequence right away, tell the player you will talk with him or her after you think about it. You might consider involving the player in designing a consequence.

- Once the discipline is completed, don't make athletes feel they are "in the doghouse." Make them feel that they're valued members of the team again.

- Make sure that what you think is discipline isn't perceived by the athlete as a positive reinforcement—for instance, keeping a player out of doing a certain drill or portion of the practice may be just what the athlete desired.

- Never discipline athletes for making errors when they are playing.

- Never use physical activity—running laps or doing push-ups—as discipline. To do so only causes athletes to resent physical activity, something we want them to learn to enjoy throughout their lives.

- Discipline sparingly. Constant discipline and criticism cause athletes to turn their interests elsewhere and to resent you as well.

chapter 6

Game-Day Coaching

Contests provide the opportunity for your players to show what they've learned in practice. Just as your players' focus shifts on contest days from learning and practicing to competing, so your focus shifts from teaching skills to coaching players as they perform those skills in contests. Of course, the contest is a teaching opportunity as well, but the focus is on performing what has been previously learned.

In the last chapter you learned how to teach your players hockey tactics and skills; in this chapter we'll help you coach your players as they execute those tactics and skills in contests. We'll provide important coaching principles that will guide you throughout the game day — before, during, and after the contest.

Before the Contest

Just as you need a practice plan for what you're going to do each practice, you need a game plan for what to do on the day of a game. Many inexperienced coaches focus only on how they will coach during the contest itself, but your preparations to coach should include details that begin well before the first play of the game. In fact, your preparations should begin during the practice before the contest.

Preparations at Practice

During the practice a day or two before the next contest, you should do two things (besides practicing tactics and skills) to prepare your players: Decide on any specific team tactics that you want to employ, and discuss pregame particulars such as what to eat before the game, what to wear, and when to be at the rink.

Deciding Team Tactics

Some coaches see themselves as great military strategists guiding their young warriors to victory on the battlefield. These coaches burn the midnight oil as they devise a complex plan of attack. There are several things wrong with this approach, but we'll point out two errors in terms of deciding team tactics:

1. The decision on team tactics should be made with input from players.
2. Team tactics at this level don't need to be complex.

Perhaps you guessed right on the second point but were surprised by the first. Why should you include your players in deciding tactics? Isn't that the coach's role?

It's the coach's role to help youngsters grow through the sport experience. Giving your athletes input here helps them to learn the game. It gets them involved at a planning level that often is reserved solely for the coach. It gives them a feeling of ownership; they're not just "carrying out orders" of the coach. They're executing the plan of attack that was jointly decided. Youngsters who have a say in how they approach a task often respond with more enthusiasm and motivation.

Don't dampen that enthusiasm and motivation by concocting tactics that are too complex. Keep tactics simple, especially at the younger levels. Focus on providing support, moving continuously, spreading out the attack, and passing and shooting often.

As you become more familiar with your team's tendencies and abilities, help them focus on specific tactics that will help them play better. For example, if your team has a tendency to stand around and watch the action, emphasize moving more and spreading out the attack. If they are active and moving throughout the game, but not in any cohesive fashion, focus them on providing support by using the triangle concept (see chapter 8).

If you're coaching 12- to 14-year-olds, you might institute certain plays that your team has practiced. These plays should take advantage of your players' strengths. Again, give the players some input into what plays might be employed in a game.

Discussing Precontest Particulars

Players need to know what to do before a contest: what they should eat on game day and when, what clothing they should wear to the game, what equipment they should bring, and what time they should arrive at the rink. Discuss these particulars with them at the practice before a contest. Here are guidelines for discussing these issues.

Pregame Meal. Carbohydrates are easily digested and absorbed and are a ready source of fuel. Players should eat a high-carbohydrate meal ideally about three to four hours before a game to allow the stomach to empty completely. This won't be possible for games held in early morning; in this case, athletes should still eat food high in carbohydrates, such as an English muffin, toast, or cereal, but not so much that their stomachs are full. In addition, athletes' pregame meals shouldn't include foods that are spicy or high in fat content.

Clothing and Equipment. Instruct players to wear the following items for a game:

- Helmets
- Pads
- Mouthguards
- Team jerseys
- Sticks
- Gloves

See p. 77 for more on hockey clothing and equipment.

Time to Arrive. Your players will need to adequately warm up before a game, so instruct them to arrive 20 minutes before a game to go through a team warm-up (see "The Warm-Up" later in this chapter).

Facilities, Equipment, and Support Personnel

Two organizations provide rules and assistance for roller hockey leagues in the US. USA Roller Hockey, which is part of USA Roller Skating, is the Olympic national governing body for roller hockey, and it governs a number of leagues from local recreational leagues to Olympic and other international competitions. USA Roller Hockey provides insurance and rules; training for players, coaches, and officials; and quality control for amateur competition. USA Hockey InLine, part of USA Hockey, also plays a leading role in roller hockey in the United States. USA Hockey InLine offers education and resources for coaches, referees, and league directors; sponsors regional and national tournaments; and provides insurance and rules for sanctioned leagues. See your sport director to ensure that you know which organization's guidelines you should follow.

Condition of Ice

✔ The ice is an inch to an inch and a half thick.

✔ The playing surface is free of debris.

✔ The ice is smooth, without cuts.

✔ The ice is even and not bumpy.

Goals

✔ The nets do not have holes and are properly secured.

✔ Goal posts do not have sharp edges.

✔ Goal backs are rounded tubes.

✔ The plates are in the ice for the goal posts.

✔ The goal releases work properly.

Rink

✔ The rink is well lighted.

✔ The boards are secure, smooth, and flat.

✔ The boards have give.

✔ The gates are correctly set on their hinges.

✔ The gates are closed during play.

✔ The plexiglass is tight and in place.

✔ The rink markings are correct.

Nearby Areas

- ✔ Walkways to the ice are clear of hockey equipment.
- ✔ The off-ice practice area (gym, tennis courts, parking lot) is not slick or slippery and is clear of hockey equipment.

Adapted from LRP Publications.

Communicating With Parents

The groundwork for your communication with parents will have been laid in the parent orientation meeting, through which parents learn the best ways to support their kids'—and the whole team's—efforts on the rink. As parents gather at the rink before a game, let them know what the team has been focusing on during the past week and what your goals are for the game. For instance, perhaps you've worked on the breakout in practice this week; encourage parents to watch for improvement and success in executing this play and to support the team members as they attempt all tactics and skills. Help parents to judge success not just based on the contest outcome, but on how the kids are improving their performances.

If parents yell at the kids for mistakes made during the game, make disparaging remarks about the officials or opponents, or shout instructions on what tactics to employ, ask them to refrain from making such remarks and to instead be supportive of the team in their comments and actions.

After a contest, briefly and informally assess with parents, as the opportunity arises, how the team did based not on the outcome, but on meeting performance goals and playing to the best of their abilities. Help parents see the contest as a process, not solely as a test that's pass/fail or win/lose. Encourage parents to reinforce that concept at home.

Unplanned Events

Part of being prepared to coach is to expect the unexpected. What do you do if players are late? What if you have an emergency and can't make the game or will be late? What if the contest is rained out or otherwise postponed? Being prepared to handle out-of-the-ordinary circumstances will help you when such unplanned events happen.

If players are late, you may have to adjust your starting lineup. While this may not be a major inconvenience, do stress to your players the importance of being on time for two reasons:

○ Part of being a member of a team means being committed and responsible to the other members. When players don't show up, or show up late, they break that commitment.

○ Players need to go through a warm-up to physically prepare for the contest. Skipping the warm-up risks injury.

Consider making a team rule stating that players need to show up 20 minutes before a game and go through the complete team warm-up, or they won't start.

An emergency might cause you to be late or miss a game. In such cases, notify your assistant coach, if you have one, or the league coordinator. If notified in advance, a parent of a player or another volunteer might be able to step in for the contest.

Sometimes a game will be postponed because of inclement weather or for other reasons (such as unsafe rink conditions). If the postponement takes place before game day, you'll need to call each member of your team to let him or her know. If it happens while the teams are on the rink preparing for the game, gather your team members and tell them the news and why the game is being postponed. Make sure all your players have rides home before you leave — be the last to leave to be sure.

The Warm-Up

Players need to both physically and mentally prepare for a game once they arrive at the rink. Physical preparation involves warming up. We've suggested that players arrive 20 minutes before the game to warm up. Conduct the warm-up similar to practice warm-ups, with some brief games that focus on skill practice and stretching.

Players should prepare to do what they will do in the game: skating, passing, shooting. This doesn't mean they spend extensive time on each skill; you can plan two or three brief practice games that encompass all these skills.

After playing a few brief games, your players should stretch. You don't need to deliver any big pep talk, but you can help your players mentally prepare as they stretch by reminding them of the following:

○ The tactics and skills they've been working on in recent practices, especially focusing their attention on what they've been doing well. Focus on their strengths.

- The team tactics you decided on in your previous practice.
- Performing the tactics and skills to the best of their individual abilities and playing together as a team.
- Playing hard and smart and having fun!

During the Contest

The list you just read goes a long way toward defining your focus for coaching during the contest. Throughout the game, you'll keep the game in proper perspective and help your players do the same. You'll observe how your players execute tactics and skills and how well they play together. You'll make tactical decisions in a number of areas. You'll model appropriate behavior on the sideline, showing respect for opponents and officials, and demand the same of your athletes. You'll watch out for your athletes' physical safety and psychological welfare, in terms of building their self-esteem and helping them manage stress and anxiety.

Proper Perspective

Winning games is the short-term goal of your hockey program; helping your players learn the tactics, skills, and rules of hockey, how to become fit, and how to be good sports in hockey and in life is the long-term goal. Your young athletes are "winning" when they are becoming better human beings through their participation in hockey. Keep that perspective in mind when you coach. You have the privilege of setting the tone for how your team approaches the game. Keep winning and all aspects of the competition in proper perspective, and your young charges will likely follow suit.

Tactical Decisions

While you aren't called upon to be a great military strategist, you are called upon to make tactical decisions in several areas throughout a contest. You'll make decisions about who starts the game and when to enter substitutes; about making slight adjustments to your team's tactics; and about correcting players' performance errors or leaving the correction for the next practice.

Starting and Substituting Players

In considering playing time, make sure that everyone on the team gets to play at least half of each game. This should be your guiding principle as you consider starting and substitution patterns. We suggest you consider two options in substituting players:

⊙ **Substituting Individually.** Replace one player with another. This offers you a lot of latitude in deciding who goes in when, and it gives you the greatest mix of players throughout the game, but it can be hard to keep track of playing time (this could be made easier by assigning an assistant or a parent to this task). Remember that players are to receive equal playing time.

⊙ **Substituting by Time.** The advantage here is that you can easily track playing time, and players know how long their shift is before they might be replaced.

Adjusting Team Tactics

At the 8 to 9 and 10 to 11 age levels, you probably won't adjust your team tactics too significantly during a game; rather, you'll focus on the basic tactics in general and emphasize during breaks which tactics your team needs to work on in particular. However, coaches of 12- to 14-year-olds might have cause to make tactical adjustments to improve their team's chances of performing well and winning. As games progress, assess your opponents' style of play and tactics, and make adjustments that are appropriate—that is, that your players are prepared for. Consider the following examples:

⊙ **How do your opponents usually initiate their attack?** Do they aim to use speed to attack the outside of your defense, do they attempt to split your defense up the middle, or do they dump the puck and chase it down deep in your zone? This can help you make defensive adjustments.

⊙ **Who are the strongest players on the opposing team?** The weakest players? As you identify strong players, you'll want to assign more skilled players to mark them.

⊙ **Are the forwards fast and powerful?** Do they come to the forecheck hard, or do they try to beat you with puck movement and player movement? Their mode of attack should influence how you instruct your players to mark them.

⊙ **On defense, do your opponents play a high-pressure game, or do they retreat once you've gained possession of the puck?** Either type of defense could call for a different strategy from you. Knowing the answers to such questions can help you both formulate a game plan and make adjustments during a game.

However, don't stress tactics too much during a game. Doing so can take the fun out of the game for the players. If you don't trust your memory, carry a pen and notepad to note which team tactics and individual skills need attention in the next practice.

Correcting Players' Errors

In chapter 5 you learned about two types of errors: learning errors and performance errors. Learning errors are ones that occur because athletes don't know how to perform a skill. Athletes make performance errors not because they don't know how to do the skill, but because they make a mistake in executing what they do know.

Sometimes it's not easy to tell which type of error athletes are making. Knowing your athletes' capabilities helps you to know whether they know the skill and are simply making mistakes in executing it or whether they don't really know how to perform the skill. If they are making learning errors—that is, they don't know how to perform the skills—you'll need to make note of this and teach them at the next practice. Game time is not the time to teach skills.

If they are making performance errors, however, you can help players correct those errors during a game. Players who make performance errors often do so because they have a lapse in concentration or motivation—or they are simply demonstrating the human quality of sometimes doing things incorrectly. A word of encouragement to concentrate more may help. If you do correct a performance error during a contest, do so in a quiet, controlled, and positive tone of voice during a break or when the player is on the sidelines with you.

For those making performance errors, you have to decide if it is just the occasional error anyone makes or an expected error for a youngster at that stage of development. If that is the case, then the player may appreciate your not commenting on the mistake. The player knows it was a mistake and knows how to correct it. On the other hand, perhaps an encouraging word and a "coaching cue" (such as "Remember to follow through on your shots") may be just what the athlete needs. Knowing the players and what to say is very much a part of the "art" of coaching.

Coach's and Players' Behavior

Another aspect of coaching on game day is managing behavior—both yours and your athletes'. The two are closely connected.

Your Conduct

You very much influence your players' behavior before, during, and after a contest. If you're up, your players are more likely to be up. If you're anxious, they'll notice and the anxiety can be contagious. If you're negative, they'll respond with worry. If you're positive, they'll play with more enjoyment. If you're constantly yelling instructions or commenting on mistakes and errors, it will be difficult for players to concentrate. Instead, let players get into the flow of the game.

The focus should be on positive competition and on having fun. A coach who overorganizes everything and dominates a game from the sideline is definitely not making the contest fun.

So how should you conduct yourself on the sideline? Here are a few pointers:

- Be calm, in control, and supportive of your players.
- Encourage players often, but instruct during play sparingly. Players should be focusing on their performance during a game, not on instructions shouted from the sidelines.
- If you need to instruct a player, do so when you're both on the sidelines, in an unobtrusive manner. Never yell at players for making a mistake. Instead, briefly demonstrate or remind them of the correct technique and encourage them.

Remember, you're not playing for the Stanley Cup! In this program, hockey competitions are designed to help players develop their skills and themselves — and to have fun. So coach in a manner at games that helps your players do those things.

Players' Conduct

You're responsible for keeping your players under control. Do so by setting a good example and by disciplining when necessary. Set team rules of good behavior. If players attempt to cheat, fight, argue, badger, yell disparaging remarks, and the like, it is your responsibility to correct the misbehavior. Consider team rules in these areas of game conduct:

- Players' language
- Players' behavior
- Interactions with officials
- Discipline for misbehavior
- Dress code for competitions

Players' Physical Safety

We devoted all of chapter 3 to discussing how to provide for players' safety, but it's worth noting here that safety during contests can be affected by how officials are calling the rules. If they aren't calling rules correctly, and this risks injury to your players, you must intervene. Voice your concern in a respectful manner and in a way that places the emphasis where it should be: on the athletes' safety. One of the officials' main responsibilities is to provide for athletes' safety; you are not adversaries here. Don't hesitate to address an issue of safety with an official when the need arises.

Players' Psychological Welfare

Athletes often attach their self-worth to winning and losing. This idea is fueled by coaches, parents, peers, and society, who place great emphasis on winning. Players become anxious when they're uncertain if they can meet the expectations of others or of themselves when meeting these expectations is important to them.

If you place too much importance on the game or cause your athletes to doubt their abilities, they will become anxious about the outcome and their performance. If your players look uptight and anxious during a contest, find ways to reduce both the uncertainties about how their performance will be evaluated and the importance they are attaching to the game. Help athletes focus on realistic personal goals—goals that are reachable and measurable and that will help them improve their performance. Another way to reduce anxiety on game day is to stay away from emotional pregame pep talks. We provided guidance earlier in what to address before the game.

When coaching during contests, remember that the most important outcome from playing hockey is to build or enhance players' self-worth. Keep that firmly in mind, and strive to make every coaching decision promote your athletes' self-worth.

Opponents and Officials

Respect opponents and officials. Without them, you wouldn't have a competition. Officials help provide a fair and safe experience for athletes and, as appropriate, help them learn the game. Opponents provide opportunities for your team to test itself, improve, and excel.

You and your team should show respect for opponents by giving your best efforts. You owe them this. Showing respect doesn't necessarily mean being "nice" to your opponents, though it does mean being civil.

Don't allow your players to "trash talk" or taunt an opponent. Such behavior is disrespectful to the spirit of the competition and to the opponent. Immediately remove a player from a contest if he or she disobeys your orders in this area.

Remember that officials are quite often teenagers—in many cases not much older than the players themselves. The level of officiating should be commensurate to the level of play. In other words, don't expect perfection from officials any more than you do from your own players. Especially at younger levels, they won't make every call, because to do so would stop the contest every 10 seconds.

After the Contest

When the game is over, join your team in congratulating the coaches and players of the opposing team, then be sure to thank the officials. Check on any injuries players sustained and let players know how to care for them. Be prepared to speak with the officials about any problems that occurred during the game. Then hold a brief Team Circle, as explained in a moment, to ensure your players are on an even keel, whether they won or lost.

Winning With Class, Losing With Dignity

When celebrating a victory, make sure your team does so in a way that doesn't show disrespect for the opponents. It's fine and appropriate to be happy and celebrate a win, but don't allow your players to taunt the opponents or boast about their victory. Keep winning in perspective. Winning and losing are a part of life, not just a part of sport. If players can handle both equally well, they'll be successful in whatever they do.

Athletes are competitors, and competitors will be disappointed in defeat. If your team has made a winning effort, let them know that. After a loss, help them keep their chins up and maintain a positive attitude that will carry over into the next practice and contest.

Team Circle

If your players have performed well in a game, compliment them and congratulate them immediately afterward. Tell them specifically what they did well, whether they won or lost. This will reinforce their desire to repeat their good performances.

Don't criticize individual players for poor performances in front of teammates. Help players improve their skills, but do so in the next practice, not immediately after a game.

The postgame Team Circle isn't the time to go over tactical problems and adjustments. The players are either so happy after a win or so dejected after a loss that they won't absorb much tactical information immediately following a game. Your first concern should be your players' attitudes and mental well-being. You don't want them to be too high after a win or too low after a loss. This is the time you can be most influential in keeping the outcome in perspective and keeping them on an even keel.

Finally, make sure your players have transportation home. Be the last one to leave in order to help if transportation falls through and to ensure full supervision of players before they leave.

chapter 7

Rules and Equipment

This is where we'll introduce you to some of the basic rules of hockey. We won't try to cover all the rules of the game but rather will give you what you need to work with players who are 8 to 14 years old. We'll give you information on the differences between ice and roller hockey, game length and number of players, rink size and markings, equipment, player positions, actions to start and restart the game, penalties, and scoring. In a short section at the end of the chapter we'll show you the officiating signals for hockey.

First, though, we'll begin by defining some terms you'll need to know to understand and teach hockey.

Terms to Know

Hockey has its own vocabulary. Being familiar with common terms will make your job easier.

attempt to injure (deliberate injury)—An infraction resulting from a player or team official attempting to hit an opposing player, team official, or game official with the intent to cause injury.

back-checking—Attempts by forwards after losing possession of the puck/ball to slow or stop opponents' offensive attack.

boarding—An infraction resulting from a player checking an opponent violently into the boards. At the discretion of the referee, players shall be penalized, based upon the degree of violence of the impact with the boards, if they body check, cross-check, elbow, charge, or trip an opponent in a manner that causes the opponent to be thrown violently into the boards.

body checking—Intentional use of the body or part of the body to hinder an opponent. Body checking is prohibited in ice hockey for boys 10 years and younger, all girls' and women's classifications, and in roller hockey.

breakaway—A scoring opportunity that exists when players with full control of the puck/ball have no opposing players between themselves and the opposing goal.

broken stick—A stick that the referee deems unfit for play.

butt-ending—An infraction resulting from a player using the shaft of the stick above the upper hand to jab or attempt to jab an opposing player.

captain—A player, other than a goalkeeper, selected to represent the team with the officials.

charging—Taking more than two steps or strides to make contact with an opposing player.

creases—An enclosed space designated for the goalkeeper's protection and the referee's use. The lines which designate this space are considered part of the crease.

cross-checking—An infraction resulting from a player, holding the stick with both hands, checking an opponent by using the shaft of the stick with no part of the stick on the surface.

deke—A fake accomplished by moving the puck/ball or part of the body to one side, then moving in the opposite direction.

delayed offsides—A situation arising when an attacking player has preceded the puck/ball across the attacking blue line, but the defending team has gained possession of the puck/ball and is in position to bring it out of the defending zone without delay or contact with an attacking player.

dribbling—Another term for handling the puck/ball.

elbowing—An infraction resulting from a player using the elbow in any way to foul the opponent.

faceoff—The action of the referee dropping the puck/ball between the sticks of two opposing players to start or resume play. A face-off begins when the referee indicates location of the faceoff and ends when the puck/ball has been legally dropped.

forwards—A collective term for the center and wingers, who have the primary offensive objective of scoring a goal.

game disqualification—The result of a serious infraction in which a player is ejected from a game. This player must leave the area of the player's bench and may in no way direct, coach, or assist the team in any manner for the remainder of the game.

game suspension—The result of a serious infraction in which a player, coach, or manager is ineligible to participate in the next scheduled game.

HECC—An acronym for the Hockey Equipment Certification Council, an independent organization responsible for the development, evaluation, and testing of performance standards for protective ice hockey equipment.

heel of the stick—The point at which the shaft of the stick and the bottom of the blade meet.

high-sticking—An infraction resulting from a player carrying any part of the stick above the normal height of the waist.

holding—An infraction resulting from a player impeding the progress of an opponent.

hooking—An infraction resulting from a player using the stick blade in a pulling or tugging motion to impede the progress of an opponent.

icing—A stoppage of play that occurs when a team sends the puck down the length of the ice from its side of the red line.

kicking—An infraction resulting from a player deliberately using the skate(s) with a kicking motion to contact an opponent, with no intent to play the puck/ball.

kneeing—An infraction resulting from a player using the knee in any way to foul the opponent.

minor official—Officials appointed to assist the on-surface officials in conducting the game, including scorer, game timekeeper, penalty timekeeper, and goal judges.

offsides—An infraction resulting from players of an attacking team preceding the puck/ball into the attacking zone.

on-surface officials—Referees.

penalty—The result of an infraction of the playing rules by a player or team official.

penalty-killing unit—A group of players brought in to defend against a power play.

players—Members of the team physically participating in a game. The goalkeeper is considered a player unless rules specify otherwise.

poke checking—A sudden move goalkeepers make with the stick to contact the puck/ball with the stick blade.

possession—The state of a player other than a goalkeeper who has most recently come in contact with the puck/ball.

power play—A situation in which one team gains a numerical player advantage, usually following a penalty.

power-play goal—A goal scored while the opponent is skating a player down for a minor penalty.

protective equipment—Equipment worn by a player for the sole purpose of protecting against injury.

shorthanded—A condition in which a team is below the numerical strength of its opponent on the surface.

slashing—An infraction resulting from a player hitting an opponent with the stick while holding the stick with one or both hands. A player who swings the stick at an opponent without making contact is still guilty of slashing.

spearing—An infraction resulting from a player poking or attempting to poke an opponent with the toe of the stick blade while holding the stick with one or both hands.

stick checking—A technique involving players' use of the stick or blade to poke or strike an opponent's stick blade or a puck/ball in an opponent's possession.

team officials—Managers and support personnel, such as team manager, coach, assistant coach, trainer, equipment manager, and statistician.

walkout—Stepping away from the boards with the puck and skating toward the area in front of the goal.

Coaching Hockey: Worth a Shot

Hockey is exciting, fast growing, and, most of all, a fun game to play. Hockey comes from Canada and is thought to be its national sport (actually lacrosse is Canada's national sport). Hockey's popularity has increased recently, and more children are expressing an interest in playing some form of the game. This book refers to two forms of hockey. One is traditional, ice hockey, and the other is the newcomer, roller hockey, or in-line hockey. We prefer to use the term roller hockey because of the roots of the sport. Roller hockey was developed and is still played today in New York, using the traditional quad or fourwheel skate, but today the in-line skate is more popular.

Throughout the United States, youth ice hockey is governed by USA Hockey, from the mite division (9-year-olds and under) to the U.S. Olympic team. USA Hockey is responsible for team insurance, rules, training of both players and officials, and quality control of the amateur game. On a professional level, the National Hockey League (NHL) reaches out to ice hockey players in North America and Europe. The NHL can be seen in most major markets in North America, and some of its members are excellent role models for young athletes. The NHL, which is closely involved with youth programs throughout North America, readily assists new coaches.

USA Roller Hockey is the Olympic national governing body for roller hockey, and it governs a number of leagues from local recreational leagues to Olympic and other international competitions. Like USA Hockey, USA Roller Hockey provides insurance and rules; training for players, coaches, and officials; and quality control for amateur competition. USA Hockey InLine, which is part of USA Hockey, also plays a leading role in roller hockey in the United States. USA Hockey InLine offers league and team memberships, as well as help in establishing new leagues, and it provides insurance and rules for teams. See your sport director to ensure that you know which organization's guidelines you should follow.

Differences Between Ice and Roller Hockey

The skating ability of beginning roller hockey players is generally slightly more advanced than that of beginning ice hockey players. Roller hockey players can practice on the driveway, street, or basement floor, but ice hockey players must either wait for freezing temperatures or for someone to take them to an ice rink. Table 7.1 shows other major differences between the two sports. Four-on-four play, no offsides, no neutral zone, no clearing (icing), and a concentration on offense are some of the differences that allow roller hockey to be a wide open, high-scoring game.

Table 7.1	Differences Between Ice and Roller Hockey	
Category	**Ice hockey**	**Roller hockey**
Number of players playing at one time/team	Five plus a goalie	13 years old and under—five plus a goalie; 13 years old and over—four plus a goalie
Object played with	Standard size and weight puck	A ball or several different types of pucks
Offside lines	Blue line	Center line or blue line or no offside
Sending the puck/ ball the length of the surface	Icing	Clearing
Goal dimensions	Standard 4' x 6'	4' x 6' for tournaments or alternate size for leagues
Rink markings	See Figure 7.1	See Figure 7.2
Rink sizes	Min. 185' x 85' Max. 200' x 100'	Min. 145' x 65' Max. 200'x 100'
Number of periods	Three	Two, three, or four

USA Hockey has established the age classifications shown in table 7.2 for all ice hockey teams playing under its rules.

Roller hockey age divisions vary significantly from league to league. USA Roller Hockey age classifications run as follows: 8 and under, 10 and under, 12 and under, 14 and under, 16 and under, and 18 and under. USA Hockey InLine has established these age classifications for its teams: 10 and under, 12 and under, 14 and under, and 17 and under.

Table 7.2 **USA Hockey Age Classifications**	
Boys	**Girls**
8 or under (Mites)	
10 or under (Squirts)	10 or under
12 or under (Peewees)	12 or under
14 or under (Bantams)	15 or under
17 or under (Midgets)	19 or under

Rules

Like any other game, hockey needs rules to keep the game safe. Unfortunately, ice hockey rules have become a bit confusing, and in roller hockey the "rules" are more like a set of guidelines. The best way to understand the rules fully is to take a referee class, which helps you not only to keep up with the rules, but also to understand what officials go through during a game. Be sure to check with your local sports organization for any rule modifications they may use.

Length of the Game

Ice and roller hockey differ in the amount of game time allotted. Usually the determining factor is the rink schedule. If the rink is dedicated to other activities (e.g., public skating), as so many are, then the total time needed to complete the game is more important than the game-playing time. For instance, if a team receives 1 hour to play a game, the rink will probably be available only for 1 hour. Typically, youth ice hockey games require 1 1/2 hours, and roller hockey games require 1 hour of available rink time.

Ice hockey rules establish the regulation time for a game as three 20-minute periods with a rest intermission between periods. Most ice hockey games are played with a stop-time clock: At every whistle the clock stops, and when the puck is dropped, the clock resumes. For younger players, a running-time clock is acceptable. The clock stops only for time-outs, injury, or rink repair. Generally, determine the actual time needed to complete a stop-time game by doubling the stop time. For example, if you were playing 15-minute periods in stop time, then you would need 90 minutes to complete a game (15 min/period $\times$ 3 = 45 min actual playing time $\times$ 2 = 90 min), with minimal rest intervals between periods. Each team is allowed a single 1-minute time-out per game.

Some roller hockey leagues have adopted the ice hockey format explained previously. USA Hockey InLine suggests that a game have two 15- to 25-minute halves, with a 2-minute rest period between halves. Each team is allowed a single 1-minute time-out per game. USA Roller Hockey recommends two 15-minute halves, with a 3-minute rest period between halves. Each team gets one 1-minute time-out per half.

Tied games in both ice and roller hockey may remain tied at the end of regulation play, be extended for one or more periods of sudden death play, or be determined by a shoot-out. In a shoot-out, a predetermined number of players from each team goes in on the goalkeeper one-on-one until there is a goal advantage for one team. This is probably the most exciting way to end a game from a fan's point of view, but from a hockey purist's view, not the fairest. The hockey purist would prefer to see the game end in a tie or to play a full overtime period to decide the game's outcome.

The Team

An ice hockey team may contain a maximum of 18 players, plus no more than two goalkeepers. By USA Hockey InLine rules, a five-on-five roller hockey team roster may contain a maximum of 15 players, plus no more than two goalkeepers; by USA Roller Hockey rules, the roster may include 12 floor players plus two goalkeepers.

Whenever possible, all teams should be dressed in the same color and style jersey, socks, and pants. Each jersey should be numbered so that there is only one of each number per team. A starting lineup must be given to a referee or scorer prior to the start of the game. Any players who are not listed will not be allowed to participate in the game, no matter when they arrive.

Rink

Rink dimensions vary so widely that it is impossible to list every option. Roller hockey rinks vary even more than their ice hockey counterparts. We have tried to list minimum and maximum sizes for ice and roller hockey rinks. If you have any questions about requirements for your rink, call the appropriate organization (USA Hockey, USA Hockey InLine, or USA Roller Hockey).

Ice Hockey

Ice hockey is played on an ice surface known as a rink. Generally, the rink should be 200 feet long and 100 feet wide. Variations in the size rink you are playing on usually are fine unless you want to host a major tournament or game; then the dimensions cannot be less than 185 feet long by 85 feet wide. The rink is surrounded by a wooden or fiberglass wall or fence known as the boards. The boards are at least 40 inches but not more than 48 inches high.

The rink is divided into three parts by two blue lines. There's also one red line through the middle. The blue lines divide the surface into a defending zone, a neutral zone, and an attacking zone. The red line divides the surface into two equal parts and is used to determine icing, which is a stoppage of play that occurs when a team sends the puck down the length of the ice from its side of the red line. The neutral zone is the area between the two blue lines that includes the center line.

Two goals are located a minimum of 12 feet to a maximum of 15 feet from each end of the rink. Each goal must be 6 feet wide and 4 feet high and include a net attached to the frame. A goal line should be drawn across the opening of the goal and continue across the surface extending from each goal post. For a goal to be scored, the puck must cross over the goal line completely. The faceoff spots, circles, and goal creases are identified in Figure 7.1.

Roller Hockey

Roller hockey is also played on a rink, either outdoors or enclosed within an indoor facility. By USA Hockey InLine rules, the dimensions are

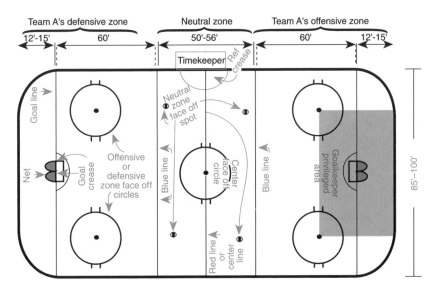

Figure 7.1 Ice hockey rink.

typically 185 feet long and 85 feet wide, but must be a minimum of 145 feet long by 65 feet wide. The rink is surrounded by a bordering material known as the boards, which extends neither less than 8 inches nor more than 48 inches above the playing surface. By USA Roller Hockey rules, the rink can be between 65 and 100 feet wide and 130 to 200 feet long, as long as the width-to-length ratio is 1:2.

For USA Hockey InLine, the rink is divided into two halves by a center red line. A team's goal area is called the defending zone, and the opposing team's area is called the attacking zone.

The official size of the goal net is 6 feet wide and 4 feet high. The goals should be placed 12 to 15 feet from the end of the rink. A goal line should be drawn across the opening of the goal and continue across the surface extending from each goal post. The faceoff spots, circles, and goal creases are identified in Figure 7.2.

For USA Roller Hockey, the rink is marked with five faceoff spots, one in the center and two at either end. The goal crease areas also are marked.

The official size of the goal net is an inside height of 41 inches and inside width of 67 inches. The goals are placed from 9 to 11 feet from the end of the rink. The faceoff spots and goal creases are shown in figure 7.2.

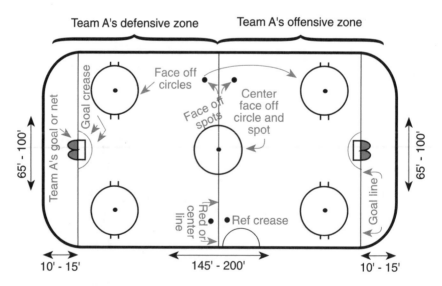

Figure 7.2 Roller hockey rink.

Equipment

Both ice and roller hockey players may try to modify equipment to enhance their play, such as adjusting the curvature of a stick. As a coach, you must be responsible for your players and ensure that they play within the equipment guidelines established by your league or governing body.

New coaches and parents need to understand the importance of proper fitting gear. Ill-fitting equipment can hinder the movements of the player, thereby creating a safety hazard as well as decreasing the player's enjoyment of the sport.

Ice Hockey

In ice hockey, the shaft of the stick should not exceed 63 inches in length, and the blade should be no more than 12 1/2 inches long. The width of the blade should be neither more than 3 inches nor less than 2 inches at any point. Curvature is generally restricted to 1/2 inch, but restrictions may vary among leagues. Check with your league administrator for rules applying to your team. The blade of the goalkeeper's stick should not be more than 3 1/2 inches wide at any point except the heel, where it must not exceed 4 1/2 inches. The blade cannot exceed 15 1/2 inches in length from the heel to the end of the blade. The widened portion of the goalkeeper's stick, extending up the shaft, can neither extend beyond 26 inches in length nor 3 1/2 inches in width.

All players must wear hockey skates with designs approved by the Rules Committee. USA Hockey recommends that skate blades be approved for ice hockey by the Hockey Equipment Certification Council (HECC), an independent organization responsible for the development, evaluation, and testing of ice hockey equipment.

All players (except those in the Senior classification) are required to wear an HECC-approved helmet and face mask. USA Hockey also recommends a full face mask, shin pads, elbow pads, hip pads or padded hockey pants, shoulder pads, tendon pads, and a protective cup (males). Most youth players are required to wear an internal mouthguard. Additional equipment may be needed for goalkeepers.

Roller Hockey

Roller hockey stick dimensions are similar to those for ice hockey; check with your organization for specific requirements.

USA Hockey InLine requires roller hockey players under 18 to wear the following equipment: head protection (hockey helmet), face protection (full face mask with a chin cup), mouthguard, elbow pads, hockey gloves, and knee and shin protection. Recommended equipment includes hip pads, padded hockey pants, protective cup or pelvic protector, chest protection, shoulder pads, and a throat protector. Goalkeepers must wear chest protection.

USA Roller Hockey requires all players to wear helmets; players 18 and under must wear full-face protection. All players must also wear shin guards, gloves, a mouthpiece, and a protective cup (males). Goalies must wear an HECC-approved mask. Eyeglass wearers must have plastic lenses, not glass.

Because specific requirements may vary, check with your director to ensure that your players' equipment meets league standards.

Table 7.3 lists equipment required for ice and roller hockey.

Table 7.3 Ice and Roller Hockey Equipment

Equipment	Ice hockey	Roller hockey
Helmet and face mask	Yes	Yes
Chin strap	Yes	Yes
Mouthguard	Yes	Yes
Elbow pads	Yes	Yes
Skates	Yes	Yes
Stick	Yes	Yes
Jersey	Yes	Yes
Shin pads	Yes	Yes
Gloves	Yes	Yes
Shoulder pads	Yes	Optional
Hockey pants or hip pads	Yes	Yes
Suspenders	Optional	Optional
Socks	Optional	Optional
Neck guards	Optional	Optional
Cup and supporter (males)	Yes	Yes

Mouthguard

Helmet (face mask & chin strap)

Gloves

Shoulder pads

Neck guard

Elbow pads

Cup and supporter

Jersey

Stick

Hockey pants

Shin pads

Suspenders

Skates

Socks

Figure 7.3 Ice and roller hockey equipment.

Player Positions

One of the hardest concepts for coaches to teach players, especially beginners, is that everyone cannot merely skate around and chase the puck/ball. The best way to teach a team a positional plan is to teach all positions to all players. This approach will take some time, but the rewards will be well worth it. Don't forget to use the classroom to start this process. A classroom, chalkboard, and the Xs and Os are some of your best coaching tools!

Ice Hockey

Each team fields five players plus a goalkeeper. Traditionally, there is one center, a left wing, a right wing, a left defensive player, and a right defensive player. Figure 7.4 illustrates the standard opening faceoff. The center has the responsibility to take most of the faceoffs and be the quarterback, while the wingers support the center and help move the puck down the ice. Figure 7.5 shows the offensive lanes that the center and wings are responsible for while on offense. On defense the center's responsibility is helping defend in front of the net. The wingers skate in their lanes (see Figure 7.6) back-checking in the neutral and offensive zones. When they enter the defensive zone, they cover the opposing defensive players up high (near the blue line). On offense, the defensive players initiate the breakout of the defensive zone and stay just inside the blue line in the offensive zone (see Figure 7.7). On defense,

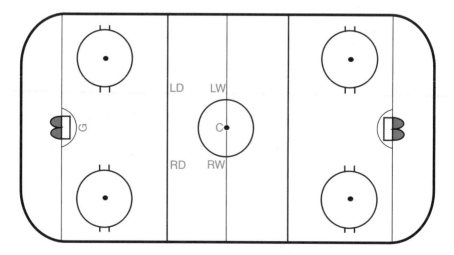

Figure 7.4   Ice hockey (five-on-five) opening faceoff.

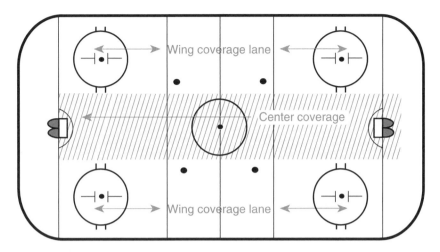

Figure 7.5   Ice hockey offensive lane coverage for forwards.

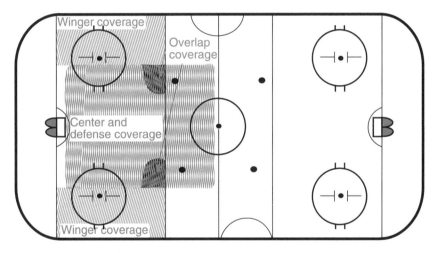

Figure 7.6   Ice hockey defensive lane coverage for forwards.

the defensive players go into the corners and cover the opposition in front of the net (see Figure 7.8). Some coaches teach that no one ever chases the opposition behind its own net. Instead the team defends in front of it and watches for a pass out in front of the net.

Roller Hockey

Each team fields either four or five players plus a goalkeeper. If the age division fields five skaters, the previous ice hockey formations and

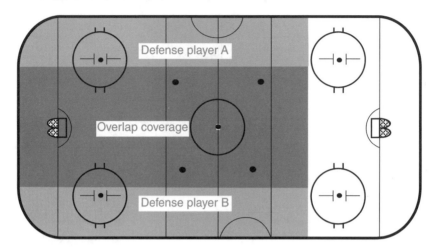

Figure 7.7   Ice hockey offensive lane coverage for defensive players.

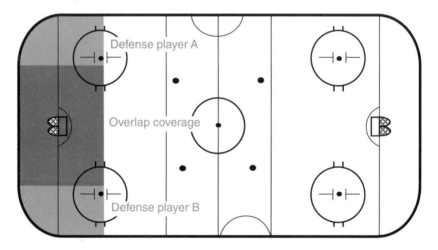

Figure 7.8   Ice hockey defensive lane coverage for defensive players.

responsibilities are the same for roller hockey. When a team fields four skaters, however, the traditional ice hockey formation no longer fits. The standard four-on-four formation of players includes one center, a left and right wing, and a defensive player. Figure 7.9 illustrates the standard opening faceoff. The offensive responsibilities of the players do not change from the previously mentioned ice hockey positions.

The defensive responsibilities change due to the lack of the second defensive player. Therefore, most teams have the second player back (no matter who it is) become the second defensive player, and then the

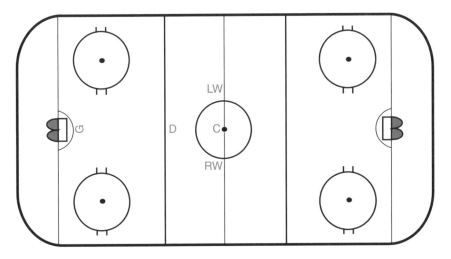

Figure 7.9 Roller hockey (four-on-four) opening faceoff.

center and the other player cover the opposition's defensive player up high. The defensive player's and center's responsibilities do not change from the previously described ice hockey coverage.

Goalkeepers in both ice and roller hockey are not restricted to staying in the net, but they also are not allowed to play beyond the offensive side of the red line. Most goalkeepers stay in their crease where they are allowed to fall on or freeze the puck/ball. Goalkeepers are the only players allowed to cover the puck/ball with their hands.

Starting and Restarting the Game

In ice and roller hockey, the game begins with a center faceoff, and each period or half is started in similar fashion. A center faceoff is also held after each goal is scored. A faceoff is the action of the referee dropping the puck/ball between the sticks of two opposing players to start or resume play. Players facing off must stand facing opposite ends of the rink (toward the opposition's goalkeeper), approximately one stick length apart, with the blades of their sticks touching the surface of the rink. No other players should be allowed within the faceoff circle until the puck/ball has been dropped by the referee. Once the puck/ball is dropped, the clock resumes (if playing with a stop-time clock).

A stoppage of play results when a referee or linesperson blows the whistle for whatever reason. At no other time, except when a goal is scored, do players stop playing without the sound of a referee's whistle. (USA Hockey occasionally changes this rule. Some years a whistle is blown for a goal and some years it is not. Be aware of your local rules.) Some of the reasons why a referee would blow the whistle are

- a player in the opposing team's crease (if not pushed or held there by an opposing player);
- a puck/ball shot out of the rink;
- a penalty called by an official;
- the end of the period;
- a puck/ball covered by the goalkeeper;
- a puck/ball lodged on the back or top of the net;
- a puck/ball lodged in someone's clothing; and
- offsides and icing (clearing in roller hockey).

For a beginning coach it is not essential to know where the faceoffs for stoppages occur, but you should know that there are offensive and defensive faceoffs, each of which is important for different reasons. The offensive faceoff is important because it is the only time you can stop and position your players for an advantage. Figures 7.10a-b show two different offensive faceoff positions each for ice and roller hockey. Try to figure out what is happening and position your players to get the best offensive opportunity. The defensive faceoff is also very important because it is the only time that you can place your defense in a position to match the opposition.

You should teach your centers or other faceoff people not to rush into the faceoff circle but to look around to make sure everyone is in the proper position. See Figures 7.11 a-b for two different defensive faceoff positions each for ice and roller hockey. The referee cannot drop the puck/ball until the centers or face-off people are in position. Faceoffs will be further discussed in chapter 8.

Penalties

A penalty is any infraction of the rules that govern play. If the team in possession of the puck/ball commits an infraction, the referee will immediately blow the whistle, stop play, and assess a penalty. If an infraction is committed by the team not in possession of the puck/ball, a delayed penalty will be signaled. At this time, the team in possession of the puck/ball can substitute a player for its goalkeeper. The goalkeeper skates to the bench, and the substitute is allowed to join play as a regular player.

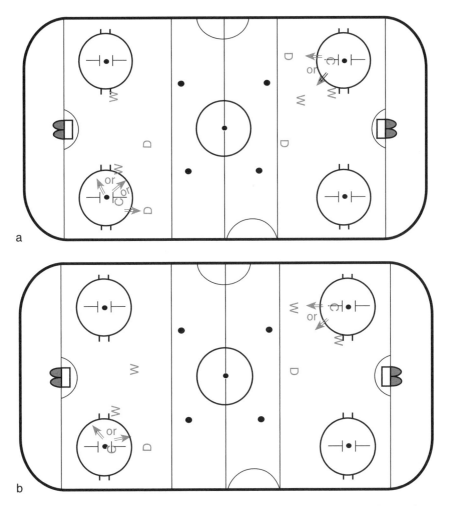

Figure 7.10 Offensive zone faceoff positions for (a) ice hockey (five-on-five) and (b) roller hockey (four-on-four).

Beginning coaches need not worry that the opposition will score by leaving the net unattended in a delayed penalty situation. Once the puck/ball is controlled by the team causing the infraction, the referee will immediately blow the whistle, stop play, and assess the penalty. There is always a chance of scoring on your own net, but this does not occur very often.

Penalties are grouped into six categories. Some infractions may have several different assessments, depending on the severity of the infraction, the intent of the player who committed the infraction, and the

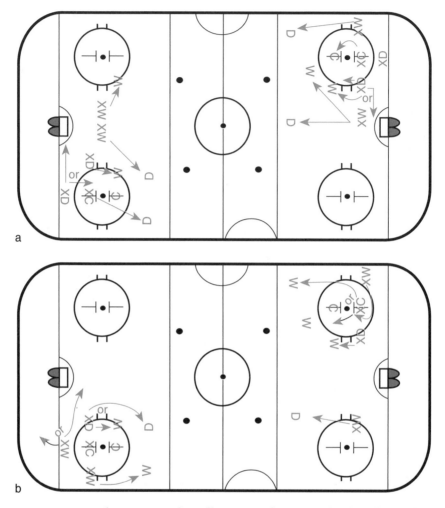

Figure 7.11 Defensive zone faceoff positions for (a) ice hockey (five-on-five) and (b) roller hockey (four-on-four).

discretion of the referee. Most ice and roller hockey penalties are similar. Table 7.4 illustrates the most common penalties for ice and roller hockey.

If a goalkeeper is assessed a minor penalty, a substitute player who was on the surface at that time will be allowed to serve the penalty for the goalkeeper, and the offending team will skate a player down. If a goal is scored by the opposing team while the offending team is skating a player down for a minor penalty (which is a powerplay goal), the offending player's penalty is over once the goal is scored, and that player

Table 7.4 Ice and Roller Hockey Penalties

Type of penalty	Penalties for ice	Penalties for roller
Minor penalties Generally: Ice = 2-min penalty Roller = 2- or 3-min penalty: 2 min for stop time and 3 min for running time	Holding, hooking, interference, tripping, delay of game, high-sticking, charging, slashing, elbowing, roughing, cross-checking, grasping the face mask, checking from behind, playing with illegal equipment, and abusing official	Holding, hooking, interference, tripping, delay of game, high-sticking, checking, slashing, elbowing, roughing, cross-checking, playing with illegal equipment, and abusing official
Major penalties Some major penalties come with a misconduct or game misconduct. Generally: Ice = 5-min penalty Roller = 5-min penalty plus in some instances a penalty shot	Cross-checking, boarding, elbowing, kneeing, slashing, checking after a whistle, checking from behind, fighting, spearing, butt-ending, attempting to injure	Cross-checking, boarding, elbowing, kneeing, slashing, checking after a whistle, grasping the face mask, checking from behind, fighting, spearing, butt-ending, attempting to injure, and boarding
Misconduct There are several types of misconduct: **General misconduct** = removal of player for 10 min without making team shorthanded	Most of the major penalties above come with a misconduct or game misconduct, also: not surrendering a stick for measurement; abusing official; mouthguard violation;	Most of the major penalties above come with a misconduct or game misconduct, also: not surrendering a stick for measurement; abusing official; mouthguard violation;

(continued)

Table 7.4 *(continued)*

Type of penalty	Penalties for ice	Penalties for roller
Misconduct (continued)		
Game misconduct = Suspension of player for rest of that game without making team shorthanded **Gross misconduct =** Suspension of player for the rest of that game without making team shorthanded with the possibility of further suspension of that player from the league	Leaving the bench during an altercation; and striking, attempting to injure,touching, or holding a game official	Leaving the bench during an altercation; and striking, attempting to injure, touching, or holding a game official
Match penalties Suspension of player for the rest of that game without making team shorthanded with further suspension of that player from the league	Attempting to injure opponent, deliberately injuring opponent, swinging stick at opponent, and taped hand cutting opponent in altercation	Attempting to injure opponent, deliberately injuring opponent, swinging stick at opponent, and taped hand cutting opponent in altercation
Penalty shot A goal instead of a penalty shot can be awarded if in the eyes of the official the puck/ball would have gone into the net.	Deliberate illegal substitution, goalkeeper deliberately displaces goal (nonbreakaway), deliberate removal of goalkeeper's helmet/ facemask, player falling on puck in crease, picking up puck in crease, throwing stick at puck in defensive end, and illegal entry into game on a breakaway	Deliberate illegal substitution, goalkeeper deliberately displaces goal (nonbreakaway), deliberate removal of goalkeeper's helmet/facemask, player falling on puck/ball in crease, picking up puck/ball in crease, throwing stick at puck/ball in

Type of penalty	Penalties for ice	Penalties for roller
		defensive end, and illegal entry into game on a breakaway
Goalkeeper's penalties Besides the regular minor penalties, a goalkeeper can receive a minor penalty for these infractions.	Wearing or playing with illegal equipment, leaving crease during an altercation, participating in play across center line, going to bench for a stick during a stoppage, piling up obstacles in front of goal cage, holding puck more than 3 seconds after warning from official, and shooting puck directly out of play	Wearing or playing with illegal equipment, leaving crease during an altercation, participating in play across center line, going to bench for stick during a stoppage, piling up obstacles in front of goal cage, holding puck/ball more than 3 seconds after warning from official, and shooting puck/ball directly out of play

is allowed to reenter play. During a major penalty, the player must serve the entire 5 minutes of the penalty, even if the opposing team scores a goal. For a second major penalty assessed to a player in a single game (goalkeeper included), a game misconduct penalty will be assessed in addition to the major penalty. That player will be suspended from play for the remainder of the game.

At the discretion of the referee, any infraction that would normally be a minor penalty can also be upgraded to a major penalty, depending on the severity and intent of the penalty. Any minor penalty infraction that causes an opponent to bleed results in the player being given a game misconduct penalty. After a misconduct penalty has expired, the player may not return to the game until there is a stoppage of play. A player who is assessed a misconduct penalty along with another penalty will serve the penalties back to back. If a substitute player is needed, that player must serve the original penalties plus all misconduct penalties. A suspension can be assessed for deliberately attempting to injure a player, which includes fighting, slashing, spearing, intentional tripping, kicking a player, and so on. Kicking a player may also lead to an automatic suspension, subject to review by the governing body of your league or organization.

A penalty shot may result from a number of infractions, ranging from interference on a breakaway to illegal substitution. Check your league rules for a complete list of these infractions. During a penalty shot, the referee will signal play to begin by blowing a whistle. The player taking the penalty shot must maintain a forward motion at all times, and the player cannot score a goal from a rebound. The goalkeeper must remain in contact with the crease area until the player taking the penalty shot makes contact with the puck/ball. If the goalkeeper leaves the crease prematurely, the referee may give the player a second chance. If no goal is scored, there will be a faceoff in the nearest faceoff spot in the defensive zone of the offending team. If the infraction that caused a penalty shot was minor, the team committing the penalty will not skate a player down when play resumes, regardless of whether a goal is scored on the penalty shot. Major, match, or misconduct penalties will be assessed in addition to the penalty shot.

Scoring

It is the responsibility of the referee—whose decision is final—to award all goals and assists. A goal is scored when the puck/ball has completely crossed the goal line. When a goal is scored, an assist is awarded to the player who passes the puck/ball to the player who scores the goal. No more than two assists are awarded per goal scored. Each goal and assist counts as one point on a player's scoring record. The referee will usually tell the official scorekeeper who scored the goal and assists, and the scorekeeper will write it down on the score sheet.

If an attacking player kicks the puck/ball directly into the net, or if the kicked puck/ball deflects off another player and/or the goalkeeper or is deliberately directed into the goal with any portion of the body other than the player's stick, the goal is disallowed. If a puck/ball deflects off an official and goes into the net, the goal also is disallowed. A goal can be scored only when the puck/ball is contacted by the player's stick below the waist.

After the game, the officials and both coaches will sign the official score sheet, and each will receive a copy. If there is any dispute over the score sheet, a coach must submit the dispute in writing to the league office.

Officiating

In both ice and roller hockey leagues, games are regulated by referees or linespeople whose main objective is to maintain control of the game and the players. They should maintain a safety-first attitude and act in a professional manner. All decisions made by referees are final.

Depending on the level of play, the number of referees and linespeople may vary, so do not be surprised if you have only one referee to officiate your games. All referees and linespeople must have some type of training, which they usually obtain by attending a certified referee clinic given by USA Hockey or USA Hockey InLine, or through USA Roller Hockey's certification program. All referees should operate under official rules governing the league. The officials should be on the surface before the teams enter and remain until all players have left the surface. Remember that the referees' presence does not alleviate your responsibility as a coach for maintaining the conduct of your team. Also keep in mind that an official may issue a penalty even after a game has ended.

Familiarize yourself with the officiating signals shown in figure 7.12 and teach them to your players.

Boarding
Striking the closed fist of the hand once in the open palm of the other hand.

Butt-ending
Moving the forearm, fist closed, under the forearm of the other hand held palm down.

Charging
Rotating clenched fists around one another in front of chest.

(continued)

Figure 7.12   Officiating signals.

Checking from behind
Arm placed behind the back,
elbow bent, forearm parallel to
the surface.

Clearing—Roller hockey
Icing—Ice hockey
Offsides
Extending the free arm (without
whistle) over the head.

Cross-checking
A forward motion with both
fists clenched extending from
the chest.

Delayed calling of penalty—ice hockey
The nonwhistle hand is extended straight
above the head.

Figure 7.12 *(continued)*

Delayed calling of penalty—roller hockey
(Penalty is one-referee system.) Referee raises arm to upright position. At stoppage of play, points with free hand (free of whistle) with palm open and fingers together.

Delaying the game
The nonwhistle hand, palm open, is placed across the chest and then fully extended directly in front of the body.

Fighting (roughing)
One punching motion to the side with the arm extending from the shoulder.

Elbowing
Tapping the elbow with the opposite hand.

Goal scored
A single point, with the nonwhistle hand directly at the goal in which the puck legally entered, while simultaneously blowing the whistle.

Figure 7.12 *(continued)*

Hand pass
The nonwhistle hand (open hand) and arm are placed straight down alongside the body and swung forward and up once in an underhand motion.

High-sticking
Holding both fists, clenched, one immediately above the other, at the side of the head.

Holding
Clasping the wrist of the whistle hand well in front of the chest.

Holding the face mask
Closed fist held in front of the face, palm in, and pulled down in one straight motion.

Hooking
A tugging motion with both arms, as if pulling something toward the stomach.

Figure 7.12 *(continued)*

Interference
Crossed arms stationary in front of chest with fists closed.

Kneeing
A single tap of the right knee with the right hand, keeping both skates on the surface.

Match penatly—Ice hockey
Pat flat of hand on the top of the head.

Misconduct
Placing of both hands on hips one time.

Figure 7.12 *(continued)*

Penalty shot
Arms crossed (fists clenched) above head.

Slashing
One chop of the hand across the straightened forearm of the other hand.

Tripping
Strike the side of the knee and follow through once, keeping the head up and both skates on the surface.

Delayed (slow) whistle
(Blueline offsides.) The nonwhistle hand is extended straight above the head. If play returns to the neutral zone withought stoppage, the arm is drawn down the instant the puck/ball crosses the line, or as soon as the offending team clears the zone.

Spearing
A single jabbing motion with both hands together, thrust forward from in front of the chest, then dropping hands to the side.

Figure 7.12   (continued)

Time-out
Using both hands to form a *T*.

Wash-out
Both arms swung laterally across the body at shoulder level with palms down. When used by the referee, it means no goal or violation so play shall continue. When used by linespeople, it means there is no icing, offside, or high-sticking violation.

Figure 7.12   *(continued)*

chapter 8

Tactics and Skills

$\mathbf{A}$s your athletes play games in practice, their experiences in these games—and your subsequent discussions with them about their experiences—will lead them to the tactics and skills they need to develop in order to succeed. In the games approach to teaching hockey, tactics and skills go hand in hand. The chapter includes games to use in your practices (see chapter 9) as well as additional games to keep your practices exciting.

In this chapter we'll provide information for you to teach your players team offensive and defensive tactics, individual offensive and defensive skills, and goalkeeping. We'll also include suggestions for identifying and correcting common errors. Remember to use the IDEA approach to teaching skills—Introduce, Demonstrate, and Explain the skill, and Attend to players as they practice the skill. For a refresher on IDEA, see chapter 5. If you aren't familiar with hockey skills, rent or purchase a video to see the skills performed. You may also find advanced books on skills helpful.

We've only provided information about the basics of hockey in this book. As your players advance in their hockey skills, you'll need to advance in your knowledge as a coach. You can do so by learning from your experiences, by watching and talking with more experienced coaches, and by studying advanced resources.

Team Tactics

Understanding individual hockey skills is important, but hockey is a team sport, and this section helps you teach individuals to play as a team. Many coaches like to say, "There is no *I* in *team*." If players follow this motto, they are more likely to play successful team hockey.

In this section, we describe team tactics in three major categories:

- Offensive play
- Defensive play
- Transitions

Teach players that when their team has the puck/ball, they all play offense, and when the opposition has the puck/ball, they all play defense. Because a primary goal of hockey is to score more goals than the opponent, teach players to put all effort into scoring a goal when they have the puck/ball and to put all effort into getting the puck/ball back when the other team has it.

In this section we also cover power plays, which occur when your team has a numerical advantage because of a penalty on the opposing team; and penalty-killing units, which are specialized groups of players who focus on defending a power play from the opposing team.

Before we begin to talk about specific team tactics, however, we need to discuss one of the most important elements of teamwork: communication.

Communication

The key to a team's ability to play together is communication on and off the rink surface. Although communication is an essential team concept, young players sometimes lack the skill to communicate effectively. For example, wanting the puck/ball, a player may stop and bang the stick on the rink surface. If he fails to receive a pass, he might bang the stick harder. You can avoid these poor communication attempts by teaching your players more effective strategies.

Verbal Communication

The easiest way to communicate is to talk. However, during a game the other team will hear, too. Teach your players to use verbal communication primarily during breaks in play. For example, players can use the break just before a faceoff to plan a strategy. If a player is always open on the left side, that player can also use the lull before a faceoff to inform a teammate.

Another good time to communicate is just after players come off the surface for a line change. Show your players how to use this bench time to discuss the last shift and plan for the next one. Also ensure that your players know how to listen, which is the most important part of communicating. One hockey coach tells his players, "You were born with two ears and one mouth. Listen twice as much as you speak, and you will have an illustrious hockey career."

Throughout the game, players should also listen closely to goalkeepers, especially when skating the puck/ball out from the defensive end. Goalies are the only players with a wide view of the open surface ahead of play. They can usually see who is open and whether the opposition is setting up on the weak or strong side.

Nonverbal Communication

Players can also use nonverbal communication, or body language. Players already use nonverbal communication in deking techniques, sending false messages to opponents by faking a move with the puck/ball one way, then following through in a different direction. Encourage them to use it with their teammates, too.

The best body parts for nonverbal communication are the eyes. Some say the eyes are the windows to the soul; in hockey they are the windows to the playbook. Players should try to make eye contact with a teammate before attempting a pass, ensuring that the player is ready. An opponent's eyes can also be revealing. It is difficult, for example, to hide fear and uncertainty. Remember, though, that players will have some difficulty making eye contact through the cage that protects the face. Players should not attempt to remove safety equipment to make eye contact.

Nodding the head can be an effective substitute if players are unable to make eye contact. Players may also point their sticks to communicate areas where they want to skate or pass.

In order for players to use nonverbal communication effectively, coaches must make sure that all the players interpret messages accurately. For example, a team could establish a signal of pointing in a specific direction for a pass, but actually wanting the pass to go in the opposite direction. Be creative, but be consistent.

Communication in Critical Situations

Two-on-One

Goalkeepers need to play the person with the puck/ball. Goalies should talk with the defense on and off the rink surface to ensure mutual understanding.

Backdoor Situations

The numerous defensive coverage exchanges and the need for quick decisions often allow a player to sneak free on the back door. Goalkeepers need to let the team know.

Screens

Goalkeepers must talk with their teammates on and off the rink surface.

Quick Breakouts

Because defensive players cannot always see what is going on behind them, goalkeepers need to communicate with defensive players.

All Other Situations

When the puck/ball is at the offensive end, goalkeepers should not fall asleep. They should keep track of game time, watch penalty time winding down, and monitor where breakouts develop. Goalies need to remember that they can see many things that the rest of the team cannot. Goalies need to communicate what they see and be positive to maintain the team's motivation.

Offensive Concepts

"What was the score?" is the most commonly asked question about a game. This section deals with the scoring aspects of hockey—that part of the game that generates the most excitement from players and fans alike. Teach these basic concepts to your players and have them filling the net:

- Make the goalie move, opening holes for shooting.
- Increase scoring productivity.
- Use one-on-one tactics.
- Read and react to teammates and opponents.

Making the Goalie Move

The number one strategy that players use to score goals is moving the puck/ball and forcing the goaltender to move. To execute this concept, players set up a play on one side of the net, then pass the puck/ball to the other side for a shot on net. To set up the play, your team enters the offensive zone in an attack triangle (see figures 8.1a-b). As players move, the attack triangle allows for support on all sides. For example, if player A in figure 8.1.a moves to a high position, then player A becomes the high support to the low players B and C (see figure 8.1b). Initially, A was the low player with support from B and C, but movement of any player changes everyone's responsibility. In five-on-five ice hockey the last two players become the final support of the triangle, forming a second triangle with one player from the first triangle (see figure 8.2a). In four-on-four roller hockey the last player into the zone forms a second triangle on the opposite side of the rink (see figure 8.2b). As players take control of the offensive zone, they try to spread out at least one of the triangles, attempting to move the goalkeeper across the net and creating the best scoring opportunity (see figure 8.3). The object of offensive play is to create high-percentage scoring opportunities. If you

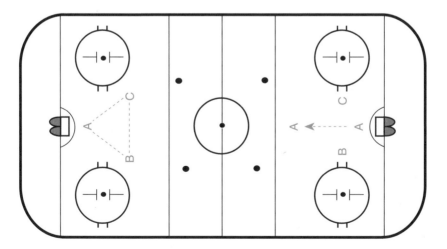

Figure 8.1   Attack triangle: (a) initial setup and (b) movement.

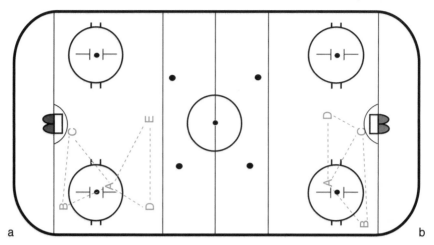

Figure 8.2   (a) Ice hockey (five-on-five) secondary triangle and (b) roller hockey (four-on-four) secondary triangle.

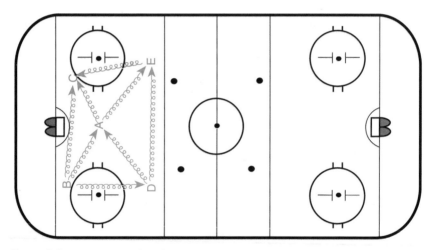

Figure 8.3   Forcing goaltender movement to create scoring opportunity.

develop players' creativity through games and tactics that create time and space, your team will enjoy more scoring opportunities.

Increasing Scoring Productivity

To increase scoring productivity, teach your players these six keys:

1. Players should anticipate and react by monitoring the goaltender's position, their own positions, puck/ball location, and opponents' and

teammates' positions. Players should look at the net before shooting and adjust the shot according to the goalie's position.

2. When in traffic, players should concentrate on shooting or creating an opportunity. Teach your players not to shoot the puck/ball when they lack good opportunities or when another player is open and in a better shooting position.

3. Players should use effective positioning to move into openings at the instant the puck/ball arrives. This concept takes some practice and a little creative skating; puck/ball races or one-on-one reverses are the best ways to improve these skills.

4. Players need to be determined. They should overcome defenders' efforts at preventing them from driving to the net, be ready for rebounds and loose pucks/balls, and avoid turning away after taking a shot on net. Some players have made it to the NHL largely because they could stand in front of the net and put rebounds in for goals. If players turn away after a shot that fails to score, they are by default giving the puck/ball to the opponents.

5. During one-on-one tactics, players should be unpredictable and develop a variety of dekes and shots. Players make opponents' jobs easy if they make the same move every time they go down the rink surface. Encourage your players to be creative and have fun.

6. Players should release the puck/ball quickly after receiving passes or making dekes. Players should avoid wasting great dekes or passes across the net by allowing the defensive team—especially the goal-keeper—to set up and react.

Using One-on-One Tactics

Help your players develop good one-on-one tactics, such as change-of-pace skating with and without the puck/ball; inside-out and outside-in skating dekes; and dekes using the head, upper body, and lower body. Also develop tactics such as faking shots, looking away before passing or shooting, driving to the net both before and after the initial shot, walkouts, and delaying. All these tactics create offensive advantages and more goals.

Reading and Reacting

Finally, you should help your players develop the ability to read and react to changing rink scenarios. The puck/ball carrier must read open rink surface, defensive pressure, and passing options and execute tactics such as those discussed previously. Teach your supporting players to decide whether to back up the puck/ball carrier, create a passing option, set a screen, or help create a numerical advantage. Also teach your players who is responsible for each of these options.

Offensive Game

10-YARD WAR

Goal

To develop the ability to beat an opponent in tight spaces.

Description

Play this game 2 v 2. Mark out a 10-by-10-yard area with cones, and designate an "endzone" for each team. (See figure 8.4.)

The object of the game is to learn to beat an opponent in a small area by using fakes, dekes, puck protection, picks, flip passes, and other creative moves. Teams attempt to get past the cones on the other side of the area of play to the "endzone." A team reaching the end zone receives a point.

To make the game easier:

⊙ Play 1 v 1.

⊙ Increase the size of the game space.

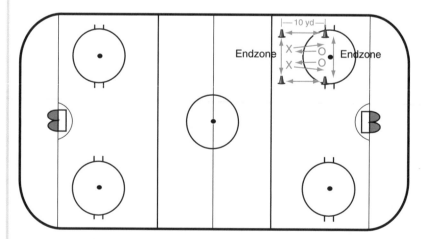

Figure 8.4   Setup for 10-Yard War.

To make the game harder:

- ◉ Play 2 v 3.
- ◉ Require at least two passes.
- ◉ Play the game along the boards (see figure 8.5). Emphasize the use of the boards as a "third player" when attempting to beat your opponent.

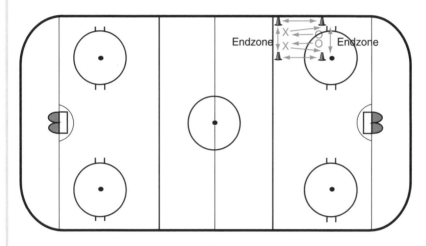

Figure 8.5 10-Yard War along the boards.

Defensive Concepts

Teach your team these basic defensive concepts to help them prevent opponents from having scoring opportunities:

- ◉ Pressure the puck/ball.
- ◉ Read and react.
- ◉ Cover in front of the net.
- ◉ Cover the points.

Pressuring the Puck/Ball

As soon as your team loses the puck/ball, one of your players should cover the puck/ball carrier, which is called pressuring. Players produce this pressure by cutting off puck/ball carriers' skating lanes, angling them into the boards, and taking away their skating surface, forcing them either to give up the puck/ball or to try to pass to a teammate (see figure 8.6). Ice hockey rules permit checking, but at younger levels and in roller hockey, players must use only stick checking.

Reading and Reacting

Once your team loses the puck/ball, players quickly assume the defensive mode, assess the situation, and attack. As in pressuring the puck/ball, players attack the puck/ball carrier first, then read and react to other players and the opponents' game plan. The closest teammate must pressure the puck/ball with defensive support. This player follows the lead of the puck/ball pressure and reacts to the action of the puck/ball carrier, looking to intercept the pass. If the opponent reaches the defensive zone, players need to force the play to the outer portion of the zone and keep the opposition, especially the puck/ball carrier, as close to the boards as possible.

Covering in Front of the Net

The opponent's offense will try to set up someone in front of your net to help with screens and try tip-ins. One of your defensive players must stay on this player in front of the net, keeping a body between the net and the offensive player's body. Remember, though, that some coaches believe that the defense should not go after the puck/ball carrier behind the net, but prepare instead for a pass or attempt to carry the puck/ball out.

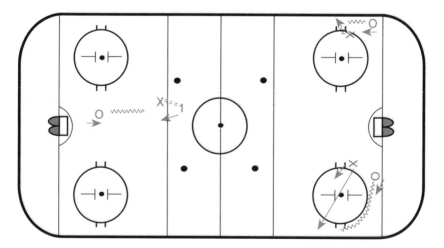

Figure 8.6   Pressuring the puck/ball: cutting off puck/ball carrier's skating space by angling the player into the boards.

Covering the Points

The other important coverage in the defensive zone—especially in a five-on-five contest—is covering the points (covering the opponent's defense person out by the blue line), by trying to stop the point person from taking shots. Remember that you are trying to regain the puck/ball before opponents enter your defensive zone and to prevent a quality shot on net. Players must be ready for the point player to deke and go around the coverage.

The Transition Game

How quickly your players transfer thoughts and actions from offense to defense, and vice versa, will dramatically affect your team's success. Ideally, ice hockey transitions from defense to offense occur in the neutral zone, and roller hockey transitions occur between the tops of the faceoff circles. Teach two primary transition concepts to your players: countering and regrouping.

Countering

If you can counter faster than your opponent can organize its attack, your team will have a good chance to regain the puck/ball quickly. Countering incorporates the element of surprise and relies on quickness to catch your opponents off guard.

Regrouping

After regaining the puck/ball with a successful counter, players must quickly regroup the team and set the offense in action. If players regroup faster than opponents counter, the team has many odd-player rushes (your offense outnumbers the opponent's defense), and odd-player rushes help you score goals.

To help players visualize the transition concept, tell them to picture offense and defense as opposite ends of a light switch. Players should strive to make transitions in the time it takes to flip the switch. Players make transitions mentally and physically, either attacking the puck/ball carrier and scrambling into prescribed defensive positions or trying to move the puck/ball toward the offensive end by scrambling into the attack triangle.

Power Plays

A power play occurs when an opponent allows your team to gain a numerical advantage, usually after a penalty. Your power-play unit, consisting of the players you decide to have on the surface during the power play, should be directed by a quarterback—the player best able to read the defense—and should be extremely quick. Before your first game, you need to develop a team philosophy for the power play: Will you use your best players or keep your same player rotation? One approach is to hold tryouts for the power-play and shorthanded (penalty-killing) units on your team (see "Penalty Killing" later in this chapter). Develop three to four different units, and practice with them all. Your power-play unit needs good passing and receiving skills: Emphasize one-touch passing, shooting, deflection, and tip-ins, and position a player who is a scoring threat in front of the net. Teach your power-play units to

1. create and master the two on one,
2. spread out the defense and move to open surface without the puck/ball,
3. develop good individual skills, and
4. address problems as they occur.

Your power-play unit should be able to read the defense, control the puck/ball, and continually move the puck/ball and opponents toward the net. If possible, practice your power-play unit against your penalty-killing unit or reserve players.

Creating and Mastering the Two-on-One

If your team outnumbers the defense two-on-one, seek a quality scoring opportunity. Teach players to stagger themselves, making it harder for the defense to cover them and forcing the goalkeeper to cover a player—usually the shooter. Also teach players to fake the shot and pass the puck/ball off the deke. Remember that the defense is trying to split your two players and force the puck/ball carrier to the outside— to prevent defenders from succeeding.

Spreading Out the Defense and Moving to Open Surface Without the Puck/Ball

During a power play, prevent defenders from covering two of your players with one of theirs. Teach players to spread out the defense by passing the puck/ball around the perimeter of the offensive zone. This allows your players to weave in and out of the space between defenders. By doing this, an offensive player can be passed the puck/ball while wide open in the middle of the defense, which can create quality scoring opportunities.

Developing Good Individual Skills

Power-play plans will succeed only if players are proficient in the basic skills such as passing and shooting the puck/ball accurately, making one-touch passes, and shooting off a direct pass. As your team's proficiency in the basic skills increases, so will the effectiveness of their power plays.

Addressing Problems As They Occur

One of the most common problems underlying ineffective power-play units is that players stand still, not moving the puck/ball. Power plays require almost constant motion. Standing still also prevents players from getting to the loose puck/ball. You can avoid this problem by allowing better-skilled, quicker players to carry the puck/ball up the surface, quarterbacking the power-play unit. Not winning faceoffs, especially in the offensive end, also causes problems: If you do not have the puck/ball, you cannot score a goal. Another problem is abandoning the attack triangle philosophy, preventing players from taking advantage of three-on-twos and support techniques. Finally, if players do not take what the opposition gives them, the power play will not succeed. Keep in mind that players frequently get in trouble by signaling their intentions, allowing the defense to prepare. Teach them to read and react!

Penalty Killing

A penalty-killing unit may be called on 6 to 15 times in a single game. You need to decide whether to prepare a specific group of players for this special situation. Very young players need to experience a variety of opportunities, but more advanced levels may increase the need to specialize.

Good penalty-killing units should possess similar skills as power-play units. Instead of focusing on scoring, though, these units focus on defending against the power play. A good penalty-killing unit should be able to read and react to the opposition and apply defensive skills effectively. One key to an effective penalty-killing unit is a good faceoff person: To control the opposition, your team must get the puck/ball. The penalty-killing unit should also be able to block shots and control play in front of its own net. Players should be quick but patient. Because you are a player down, the team must wait for an opportunity, then seize it.

When your five-on-five ice hockey team is a player down, select from two basic formations: box formation and diamond formation (see figures 8.7a-b). The disadvantage of the box formation is that the box

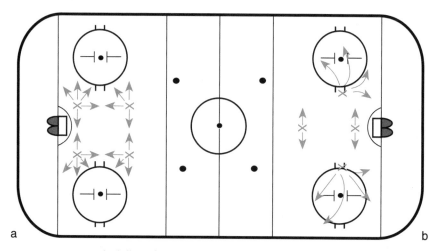

Figure 8.7 Penalty-killing formations: (a) box formation and (b) diamond formation.

can be collapsed by the opponent's offense, leading to an unorganized defense at a very vulnerable time. The disadvantage of the diamond formation is that one player has to cover the opponent's two-point players, probably leading to several long shots on net. However, if that player is your quickest and smartest, the team will also have a chance at a few shorthanded breakaways. In five-on-three ice hockey and four-on-three roller hockey (when your team is down two players), the only formation to play is a triangle (see figure 8.8). Keep the base of the triangle

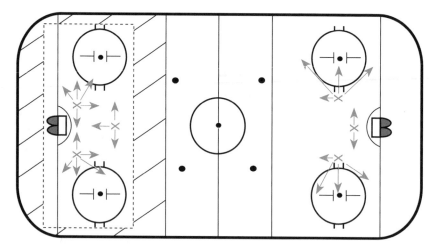

Figure 8.8 Triangle penalty-killing formation (five-on-three or four-on-three).

down by the net, as it represents the highest-percentage scoring area for the opposition. The final formation, four-on-two roller hockey, leaves your team with only two players to defend the entire surface. Your best chance is an alert goaltender and two players who are as fast as lightning. Your two players each try to cover half of the surface, usually right and left, but opponents frequently win this battle.

When a penalty-killing unit gets control of the puck/ball, it has two choices: clear the puck/ball all the way down the surface (icing is negated for a penalized team during the penalty) or try to control it by spreading out and using crisp, sharp passes, trying to play keepaway from the opposition. Depending on the opponent's momentum and the area in which your team recovers the puck/ball, each is an effective tool in killing penalties. Just remember to practice!

Fundamental Rules of Hockey by Fred Shero

- Never go offside on a three-on-two or a two-on-one.
- Except on a power play, never go backward in the defensive end unless passing back to a teammate to elude opposition.
- Never throw a puck/ball blindly out from behind the opponent's net.
- Pass diagonally in your own zone only when 100 percent certain.
- The second (support) player must go all the way for a rebound.
- Players in front of the opponent's net must face the puck/ball and lean on their sticks.
- If puck/ball carriers cross over the center of the rink with no one to pass to and no skating room, they must shoot deep into the opposition's end.
- Players should never turn their backs to the puck/ball; they should always know where it is. On a swing to the corner in their own end, defensive players may turn the back for a fraction of a second.
- Players in their own defensive zone should only be outnumbered during a penalty.
- Goalkeepers should alert everyone, usually by banging the stick on the surface, when an opponent's penalty is almost over.

Individual Skills

In chapter 4 you learned how to teach skills and plan practices. This section will help you apply that knowledge to teaching forward and backward skating; basic skills such as stick handling, passing, shooting, and stick checking; and goalkeeping.

Forward Skating

Hockey games demand too much concentration for players to be thinking about how to skate; therefore, skating is the most important skill to practice. Regular practice is the key to improving skating ability.

Three Phases of Skating

Skating involves three phases: drive, glide, and recovery.

Drive. In the drive phase, players generate power through a skating thrust to the side. The back leg extends fully, followed by a final push off the toe of the skate (see figure 8.9a).

Glide. In the glide phase, athletes maintain the body over the glide foot to maximize each stride length. Shoulders line up over the knee, which lines up over the toes (see figure 8.9b).

Recovery. In the recovery stage, players quickly bring the extended foot back under the body midline, which ensures that the hips are over the skates with each extension (see figure 8.9c).

Generation of power is called the Z: All three joints are flexed, with knees over toes, chest over knees, and head up (see figure 8.10).

Ready Position

The ready position is the building block for all skating. Just as a strong base gives a pyramid strength, the ready position provides a sturdy base for hockey players.

Players take the ready position with skates parallel and their feet shoulder-width apart, toes pointed straight ahead. Players bend the knees until they are in line with the skates' toes, lean the body slightly forward with the head up, and place one or two hands on the stick. The stick blade touches the rink surface.

Forward Striding

Players develop power with fast, short strides, then use longer and less frequent strides as speed increases. The stride starts with feet shoulder-width apart and all weight on the push foot. A player turns the push foot 35 to 40 degrees and pushes to the side and down, pressing the

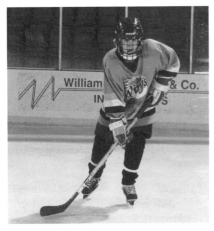

a

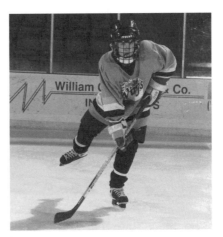

b

c

Figure 8.9 Three phases of skating: (a) drive, (b) glide, and (c) recovery.

Figure 8.10 Generation of power: the Z.

115

skate wheels or blade firmly against the rink surface. As he forces the push foot out to the side, the player pushes the knee of the other leg forward, extending the push skate leg as far as possible, through the ankle to the tip of the toe. After finishing the stride, the player transfers weight to the forward foot (glide leg) and lifts the push foot slightly over the rink surface. The player bends the knee of the back leg and pulls it forward, close to the gliding foot, keeping it close to the rink surface and placing it back in its starting position to complete the recovery phase. The player then starts the next stride with the opposite foot.

Starting Forward Striding. Teach your players two basic starts to begin a forward stride quickly and easily: the V-start and the crossover start.

For the V-start, the player starts in ready position, then turns the heels in and toes out, making a V with the skates as he leans slightly forward, putting weight on the front part of the foot. (See figure 8.11.) He starts to drive with either the right or left skate and alternates legs with each stride. The player makes the first stride with each foot a short, driving

Error Detection and Correction for Striding

ERROR Head and shoulders not moving

CORRECTION Shift weight toward the stride foot.

ERROR Chest closed and no arch in the small of the back

CORRECTION Lift the head (look straight ahead) and maintain a comfortable arch in the small of the back.

ERROR No flexion at the back of the striding knee

CORRECTION Keep a 90-degree flexion at the back of the striding knee so that the thrust leg aligns the knee over the toe of that skate.

ERROR No rhythmic and complementary arm action

CORRECTION Use a rhythmic and complementary (front to back) arm action just like a natural walking arm swing.

ERROR No power generation in thrust

CORRECTION Generate power through a skating thrust to the side and a full extension of the push leg.

stride, as if running. He makes the next two strides slightly longer and reduces the angle between the rink surface and the wheels or blades. The player's third or fourth stride should have a wheel or blade angle of 35 to 40 degrees, and he should keep his skates near the rink surface for a quick recovery phase. The player gradually straightens up as speed increases.

For the crossover start, the player starts in ready position, then turns the head and places the stick in the direction of intended travel. He then takes the outside foot and steps over the inside foot, staying low and not hopping. When the outside foot contacts the

Figure 8.11 (a) V-start initial position.

rink surface, the player must keep it on the inside edge, using it as the driving foot in the push phase. The player takes the original inside skate and places it on the rink surface near the driving skate, forming a T with the skates. Finally, the player drives with the inside edge and continues the stride.

Error Detection and Correction for Starting

ERROR Improper upper body angle

CORRECTION Keep the upper body at a 60-degree angle to the rink surface. Keep the head and chest up and pointed down the rink.

ERROR Improper starting strides in attack phase

CORRECTION Make the first two starting strides in attack phase short with external rotation of the skate as close to 90 degrees as possible.

ERROR Improper edging

CORRECTION Push off inside edges and maintain shoulder-width skate bases.

Skating Games

COPS AND ROBBERS

Goal

To develop skating quickness and agility the full length of the ice.

Description

All players are involved in this game, which uses the full length of the ice. The area behind the goal lines is designated as the safety zone. (See figure 8.12.)

Select two to four players as "cops" (CP), depending on the number of total participants. Those who are cops may not enter the safety zone. They start each round (one time down the ice) between the blue lines. Their job is to tag the "robbers" (R).

Robbers skate from goal line to goal line, attempting to avoid being touched. Those who are tagged must skate around the neutral zone with their hands in the air to signal that they have been tagged. A tagged robber can become a robber again by being tagged by a robber while his hands are in the air. Otherwise, those robbers that are tagged become cops the next round and attempt to tag the robbers.

The game ends when all robbers but one have been tagged and are now cops.

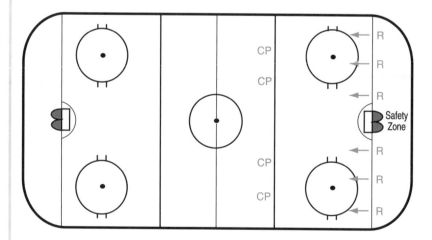

Figure 8.12   Setup for Cops and Robbers.

To make the game easier:

- ◉ Reduce the number of participants.
- ◉ Reduce the number of cops.

To make the game harder:

- ◉ Assign coaches as cops.
- ◉ Decrease the size of the safety zone.
- ◉ Reduce the size of the playing area to half-ice.

FREEZE TAG

Goal

To develop forward skating stride and agility.

Description

All players are involved in this game, which is played between the goal line and the blue line. Mark off with cones a 10-foot-by-10-foot area behind the goal line, which is the safety zone. (See figure 8.13.)

Select two to four players as "it" (I), depending on the number of total participants. Those who are it may not enter the safety zone. Their job is to attempt to tag everyone who is not it. Those who are tagged must freeze in their spots and not move until a teammate touches them. The game ends when all skaters are frozen.

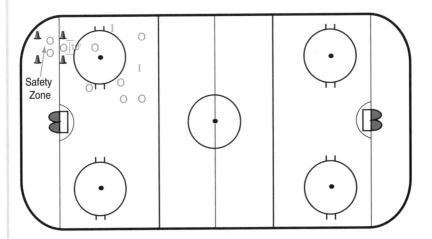

Figure 8.13 Setup for Freeze Tag.

(continued)

To make the game easier:

- ◉ Reduce the number of participants.
- ◉ Enlarge the safety zone.
- ◉ Reduce the number of its.

To make the game harder:

- ◉ Assign coaches as its.
- ◉ Decrease the size of the safety zone.
- ◉ Allow a player to be unfrozen only if a teammate slides on the ice between the frozen player's legs.

BE READY!

Goal

To develop a consistent skating ready position during a gamelike situation.

Description

Place four nets inside the offensive zone in a diamond pattern. (See figure 8.14.) All players (a maximum of 14) are involved in this game, which simulates clutter. Tell the players to scatter themselves in the offensive zone. You stand in the corner along the goal line of the offensive zone.

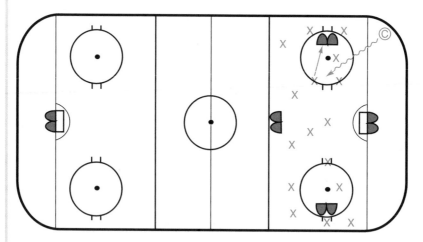

Figure 8.14   Setup for Be Ready!

The object of the game is to maintain a consistent ready position in skating. When you blow your whistle, players skate in any direction in ready position (stick on the rink) with their eyes on you (the coach). You randomly pass the puck/ball indirectly into the group of players. The player who receives the puck/ball should immediately shoot on net. Award one point for successfully receiving a pass, one point for getting a shot on goal, and one point for a goal. The player with the most points at the end of the game wins.

To make the game easier:

⊙ Reduce the number of players.

To make the game harder:

⊙ Place a second coach in the other corner of the offensive zone. This coach also randomly passes a puck/ball into the group of players.

⊙ Pass pucks/balls into the group of players more frequently.

⊙ Turn this into a 3 v 3 game by allowing the players to play until someone scores.

⊙ Use colored pucks/balls and require players to shoot a particular type of shot based on the color of the puck/ball.

ONE-FOOT FACEOFF

Goal

To develop fundamental skating motion (drive, glide, and recovery) in a gamelike situation.

Description

This is a 3 v 3 cross-rink game. Position a net 15 feet from each sideboard. (See figure 8.15.)

The object of the game is to develop players' skating stride by emphasizing the motion of one leg. Start the game by passing the puck/ball into the zone. A player enters the zone by pushing off with the left leg. A player can only push off with the left leg; the right leg must stay on the rink and cannot be used to push off. Award a team two points for skating past their opponents while puckhandling or ballhandling and one point for a goal. Play for 60 seconds, then begin a new game by blowing the whistle to end the previous game and

(continued)

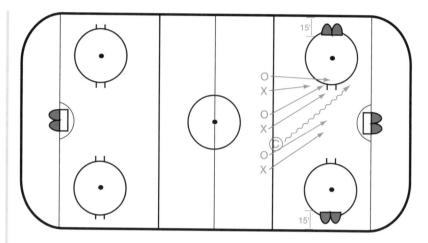

Figure 8.15   Setup for One-Foot Faceoff.

passing the puck/ball in to start the new game. Tell players to push off with the right leg in the second game.

To make the game easier:

⊙ Reduce the number of players.

To make the game harder:

⊙ Create an odd-player situation such as 2 v 3, 3 v 4, or 4 v 5.

GET UP AND GO

Goal

To develop speed and power in crossovers in a gamelike situation.

Description

This is a 1 v 1 game. The game begins from the goal line at one end. Place a second goal on the center red line, and send a goaltender to the goal at center rink. (See figure 8.16.)

The object of the game is for players to get up to their feet from the rink and skate as quickly as possible to reach the puck/ball. Have the players lie on their bellies, one at each post of the net facing the far end. Then send a puck/ball up the middle of the rink so that the players can chase it down. Players must get up and skate around the nearest faceoff circle once before pursuing the puck/ball. Players play 1 v 1 until one player scores on the net or the goalie holds the puck/

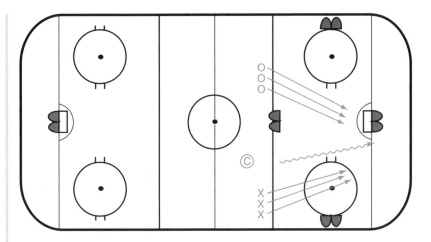

Figure 8.16   Setup for Get Up and Go.

ball. Getting to the puck/ball first is worth two points and a goal is worth one point.

To make the game easier:

⊙ Allow players to stand instead of lying on the rink.

To make the game harder:

⊙ Have the players lie on the rink facing the boards and/or with their backs on the rink.

⊙ Play 2 v 2 or 3 v 3.

⊙ Add a defensive player at the far goal to create a 1 v 2 situation for the puck/ball carrier.

⊙ Add an offensive player at the far goal to create a 2 v 1 situation for the puck/ball carrier.

Stopping Forward Striding. To become an effective hockey team, your players need to learn three basic stopping techniques: the one-foot drag, the quick turn, and the two-foot or hockey stop. One of the most important elements of stopping is the preparation phase, which will be lengthy while players learn the various stops, but will shorten as they become more proficient with their techniques.

The one-foot drag is primarily used in roller hockey. It will not stop players quickly and is better used as a slowing maneuver. To begin, a player stops skating and glides into the approach. He needs to assume the ready position and determine which foot will be the glide skate and which will do the stopping. The player should then allow the stopping skate to drag behind—not beside—the glide leg. He should drag the stopping skate on the inside edge of the wheels, placing direct pressure on it.

To execute the quick turn, the player needs to stop skating and glide into the approach in the ready position. Next, he should place the skate on the side he wishes to turn toward directly in front of the other skate in a heel-toe arrangement (if turning right, the right foot must be in front). The player leads the stop by turning the head and shoulders in the direction he wants to turn and bringing the arms and stick to the same side. Weight should be distributed as evenly as possible on both skates.

The player exerts pressure on the outside edge of the leading skate and inside edge of the trailing skate. He should avoid sitting back on the skates; he should keep the skates apart at shoulder-width around the quarter of a semicircle. Once the turn begins, the player must press down with extreme force, causing the skates to produce a quick turn. As the player stops, he will feel a force trying to propel him out of the stop, and he should be prepared to counter this force with proper body lean.

The two-foot or hockey stop maneuver is an advanced move, and the player should initially turn just to the strong side. While staying in the basic stance, the player glides on both skates as he approaches the stopping point in ready position. He must then turn the body at a right angle to the direction of travel (see figure 8.17a). The player begins the stop by turning the shoulders (see figure 8.17b), then the hips, as he swings the outside leg into braking position. The inside leg acts as a pivot, skates remain shoulder-width apart, and the inside skate travels slightly ahead of the outside skate in a heel-toe relationship. Weight is equally distributed on both skates. Next, the player extends the legs vigorously while exerting pressure on the front part of the skates, using the inside edge of the outside skate and the outside edge of the inside

a   b

Figure 8.17   Two-foot or hockey stop: (a) Turn the body at a right angle to the direction of travel; (b) begin the stop by turning the shoulders; then turn the hips and swing the outside leg into braking position.

skate. Pressure on the inside edge of the lead skate (outside skate) is especially important. Head and shoulders should remain straight, and the player should avoid looking down at the rink surface.

The player should keep both hands on the stick, but avoid leaning on it.

Error Detection and Correction for Stopping

ERROR   Improper foot placement

CORRECTION   Keep feet shoulder-width apart with heel-toe alignment of skates.

ERROR   Improper body alignment and weight transfer

CORRECTION   Take a sitting-down position with a good backward lean. Distribute weight evenly over both skates with pressure on the front of the skates.

Stopping Games

STOP AND GO

Goal

To develop stopping and changing directions during a competitive game.

Description

Play this game 3 v 3 inside the blue line. Place four nets in a diamond pattern inside the zone. (See figure 8.18.)

The object of this game is for two teams of three players to score on any of the four nets. Begin the game by passing the puck into the zone. During play randomly blow the whistle to signal the players to hockey stop immediately. Players must come to a complete stop and then immediately (without a whistle) attack the net opposite the one they were facing. Teams receive one point for a goal and four points if they hockey stop on every whistle. Begin a new game after 60 to 90 seconds.

To make the game easier:

⊙ Decrease the distance between the nets.

To make the game harder:

⊙ Require all players to touch up on the blue line on the whistle and then continue play.

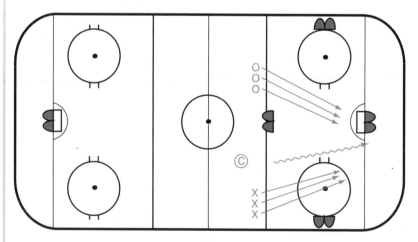

Figure 8.18 Setup for Stop and Go.

BURN AND CRASH

Goal

To develop stopping by going to the net and fighting for the rebound.

Description

Play this game 2 v 1. Place a goaltender in the net. (See figure 8.19.)

The object of this game is for offensive players to stop in front of the net and try to shoot a rebound. Two offensive players drive to the net from the blue line as you feed the puck in from the point. The offensive players hockey stop in front of the net and look for a rebound. A defensive player then enters the game from the corner to make the game 2 v 1. Coming to a complete stop in front of the net is worth one point; coming to a complete stop and scoring off the initial rebound is worth two points. Play continues until a goal is scored or the goalie freezes the puck. Any goal scored following the initial rebound is worth one point.

To make the game easier:

⊙ Make the game 2 v 0.

To make the game harder:

⊙ Make the game 2 v 2 or 2 v 3.

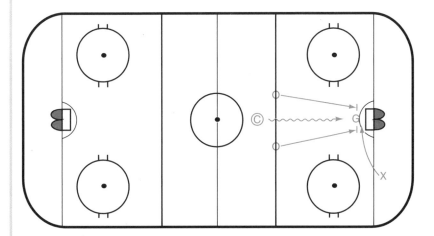

Figure 8.19   Setup for Burn and Crash.

Turning

Hockey requires players to make frequent transitions from one direction to another. Although stopping techniques are effective for changing directions, players also need to learn three methods for turning on their skates: the glide turn, the stride turn, and the crossover turn.

Glide Turn, also called the power turn. This turn is similar to stopping. A player begins a glide turn with a preparation phase. First, he stops skating and glides into an approach in ready position. The player places the skate on the side he wishes to turn toward directly in front of the other in a heel-toe relationship (see figure 8.20a). Next, the player turns the head and shoulders in the direction he wishes to turn and brings the arms and stick to the same side (see figure 8.20b). The player leans from the hips down, inside the half circle that his skates will make on the rink surface. He should distribute weight evenly over both skates, keeping pressure on the outside edge of the leading foot and inside edge of the trailing foot (see figure 8.20c).

The player should keep his skates shoulder-width apart and his center of gravity ahead of the skates to allow him to cross over after the tight turn and accelerate rapidly. Do not allow a player to sit back on his skates. Once the skates have traveled a complete half circle on the rink surface, the player executes a crossover start by bringing the back leg over the front leg to power out of the turn.

Stride Turn. The player stops skating and glides into the approach in ready position. He transfers weight over the support leg and leans into the direction of the stride, striding on the inside skate and pumping with the outside skate as if sculling. The outside edge of the glide leg and inside edge of the thrust leg propel the player through the turn,

---

Error Detection and Correction for Glide Turns

ERROR   Improper foot placement and alignment

CORRECTION   Place the inside skate ahead, leading the turn.

ERROR   Improper weight transfer and body lean

CORRECTION   Use a strong sitting-down action, lowering the body weight through the hips.

ERROR   Improper upper-body positioning

CORRECTION   Turn head and shoulders first to assist body rotation through the turn.

a

b

Figure 8.20 Glide turn: (a) Place the skate closest to the direction of the turn directly in front of the other skate in a heel-toe relationship; (b) turn the head and shoulders in the direction of the turn and bring the arms and stick to the same side; and (c) distribute weight evenly over both skates, keeping pressure on the outside edge of the leading foot and inside edge of the trailing foot.

c

and he finishes with low recovery skate placement and a strong toe-kick action.

Crossover Turn. The player uses the crossover turn to maintain or increase speed while turning. First, the player pushes the outside skate to the side, maintaining contact with the rink surface until the leg is fully extended. At the end of the push, the player pushes down on the ball of the foot, using the ankles to get a little extra push from each stroke. The player leans into the turn from the waist down, pushing the hips into the turn and keeping the inside shoulder up. After the extension, the player swings the outside leg over the inside skate. The outside skate should be parallel to the inside skate and slightly ahead of it. The player then pushes the inside skate to full extension outward under the body, using the outside edge. Once the skate is fully extended, it is returned quickly to its original position under the body, beside the outside skate. The player repeats this sequence throughout the turn, using equal force with each stroke. Players should practice this maneuver in both directions.

Error Detection and Correction for Crossover Turn

ERROR   Problem staying in turn

CORRECTION   Start with a glide turn using a strong sitting-down action. Keep the stick to the inside of the turn and use the head and shoulders to assist body rotation.

ERROR   Lack of power

CORRECTION   Bend the knee of the glide foot and fully extend the push foot.

Turning Game

FOUR-GOAL GAUNTLET

Goal

To develop turning during a competitive game.

Description

Play this game 2 v 2. Place four nets inside the neutral zone, with the opening of each net facing the boards. (See figure 8.21 for the configuration of the nets.)

The object of this game is for the teams to score on any one of the four nets. The game begins with the puck on the center rink faceoff dot. Play occurs inside the neutral zone, with teams allowed to score on a particular net only once. The game is to four points, with a goal counting one point.

To make the game easier:

⊙ Decrease the distance between the nets.

⊙ Face the goals toward center ice. However, require players to score on the goal opposite the one they were facing when their team first received the puck.

To make the game harder:

- ◎ Make the game 3 v 2 to create odd-person situations.
- ◎ Give teams a designated goal for bonus points. Rotate the designation of the "bonus goal" every 15 seconds.

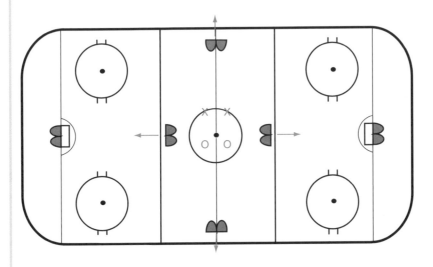

Figure 8.21   Setup for Four-Goal Gauntlet.

Pivoting

The pivot is a vital skating skill for helping your players make transitions. These transitions are especially important during games, when all players must be ready to play any position. For example, a center may be caught in a defensive player's position. Players who pivot effectively will be better prepared for these situations.

To make a forward to backward pivot, a player gains forward momentum and coasts on the left skate. The player straightens up and rotates the right skate outward (as close to 180 degrees as possible) in a near heel-down position. He starts the turn by rotating the right shoulder backward, and the torso and hips follow. The player transfers weight from the left skate to the right skate, steps down on the right skate, then takes weight off the skates by going from bent knees to straight legs. The player finishes the pivot by turning the left skate parallel with the right skate, then pushing to the side with the right skate and starting to skate backward. Teach your players to pivot to both sides.

Pivoting Game

TO THE MIDDLE

Goal

To develop the ability to pivot in a game situation.

Description

Play 2 v 2, positioning players at the goal line. Designate one team the offense and one the defense. In two separate areas, create three zones with cones, spacing the cones 15 feet apart. Use only one net positioned in the goal crease. (See figure 8.22.)

The purpose of this game is to pivot toward the middle of the rink. Players should skate forward to zone 1 and pivot to skate backward at the cone. At this time O_1 makes a cross-rink pass to O_2. Players skate backward to zone 2 and pivot to skate forward at the cone. This time O_2 passes to O_1. Finally, players pivot at zone 3 to skate backward and make one final pass. Give a team one point for pivoting to the middle in all three zones. Begin a 2 v 2 game after reaching zone 3. Continue play until the offense scores (one point) or the goaltender holds the puck/ball.

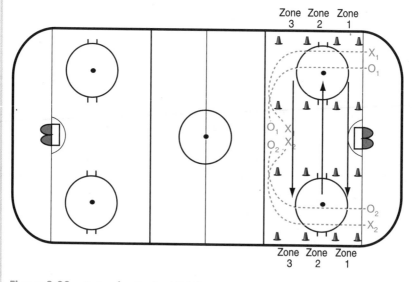

Figure 8.22 Setup for To the Middle.

To make the game easier:

- Eliminate the passes and put a puck/ball into play following entry into zone 3.

To make the game harder:

- Increase the number of players to 3 v 3.

Backward Skating

Most beginning ice and roller hockey players have problems skating backward, largely because they lean forward and bend the knees improperly. Most players need extra practice time to perfect the following backward maneuvers.

Backward Striding

The player begins in the ready position with feet close together and all weight on one foot. Using the front two wheels or the front portion of the blade, the player pushes straight out to the side until the push leg is straight. When the stride is completed, the player steps to the opposite foot and lifts the foot he has pushed with. Next, he bends the knee of the free leg and, keeping it close to the rink surface, pulls it toward the skating leg. As the free foot nears the skating foot, the player starts striding with the opposite leg. He continues this alternating action with both feet, keeping weight over the striding leg.

Push and Glide Backward

The player is moving backward with skates shoulder-width apart and all weight on one skate. Using the two front wheels or the front portion of the blade, the player pushes straight out to the side until the push leg is fully extended (see figure 8.23a). He glides while the push leg recovers to a position under the body, close to the rink surface (see figure 8.23b). The stride resembles a toe-in thrust, driven by the inside edge to form a C, which is called the C-cut of backward skating (see figure 8.23c). The player continues the alternating action with both feet, keeping weight over the striding leg.

Pivot (backward to forward)

The player begins moving backward. To turn to the left, the player first transfers weight to the right skate, then rotates the left shoulder backward. The torso and hips follow. The player lifts the left skate off the rink surface, turns it as close to 180 degrees as possible, and glides

a

b

c

Figure 8.23 Push and glide backward: (a) Push straight out to the side until the push leg is fully extended; (b) glide while the push leg recovers to a position under the body; and (c) drive stride by the inside edge to form a C.

straight back on the right skate. The player then transfers weight to the left skate to complete the turn. At the moment of weight transfer, the player must dig in the right skate and push hard, fully extending the right leg. The player is then ready to start forward striding. Teach players to accelerate out of the turn and to pivot to both sides.

Backward Crossover Stride

The player begins by moving backward with skates shoulder-width apart and weight evenly distributed over both skates. Next, he C-cuts with the lead foot and, from a ready gliding position, lifts the outside skate and steps over the inside foot. Then the player pushes off of the outside edge of the skate (power generation) and transfers the weight from the outside edge of the push foot to the inside edge of the support leg and completes the maneuver. The stepping action continues until the player is in the desired direction.

Backward One-Foot Stop and T-Push

The player begins moving backward, then extends the right leg and transfers weight to the left leg. The right leg begins to swing back, and the shoulders, hips, and legs turn in a counterclockwise direction as the player plants the right skate in a braking position, using the inside edge of the skate (see figure 8.24a). The player bends the right knee and transfers weight from the left leg to the right leg (see figure 8.24b). The majority of resistance comes from the right skate. The left skate and knee move under the body, placing the skates in position for a T-push start (see figure 8.24c).

a

b

c

Figure 8.24   Backward one-foot stop and T-push: (a) Swing the right leg back, turning the shoulders, hips, and legs in a clockwise direction, and plant the right skate in a braking position using the inside edge of the skate; (b) bend the right knee, transferring weight from the left to the right leg; and (c) move the left skate and knee under the body, placing the skates in position for a T-push start.

V-Stop for Backward Skating

The player spreads the feet shoulder-width apart with the toes of both skates turned out and heels turned in (see figure 8.25). He leans forward, forcing the inside edges of the skates against the rink surface. The player should keep a slight bend in the knees during the first phase of the stop, then extend the legs during the final phase, exerting pressure through the skates' wheels or blades. After stopping, the player should be in ready position, prepared to skate in any direction.

Figure 8.25 V-stop for backward skating.

Error Detection and Correction for Backward Skating

ERROR Improper body position

CORRECTION Hold the trunk more upright than in forward skating and flex at the hip, knee, and ankle. Maintain a good sitting-down position.

ERROR Improper weight transfer

CORRECTION Posture should allow for total body mass to be located over the ball of the foot and well within the base for support.

ERROR Improper skating stride

CORRECTION Direct force with a ball-to-heel thrust, forming a C-cut with the striding skate.

Backward Skating Games

BACKWARD BLITZ

Goal

To develop backward skating in a competitive game situation.

Description

Play this game 2 v 3. Start with two defensive players on the goal line. (See figure 8.26.)

The object of this game is for the defense to retrieve the puck and attempt to leave its defensive zone. Defensive players skate backward and stop at the defensive blue line and the red line. As the defensive players reach the second blue line, pass the puck into the zone behind them. Two offensive players forecheck the defensive players. The defensive players must pivot and retrieve the puck. A 2 v 3 game begins, with the defense receiving one point if they are able to get the puck out of the zone and two points if they are able to maintain control of the puck and leave their defensive zone. The offensive team receives one point for stealing the puck and two points for a goal. Begin a new game once the puck leaves the zone, a goal is scored, or the goalie holds the puck.

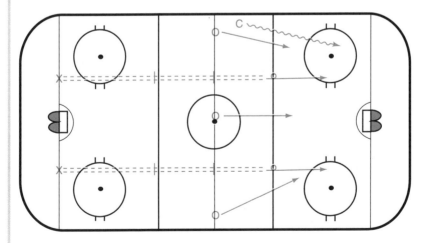

Figure 8.26   Setup for Backward Blitz.

(continued)

To make the game easier:

- Begin the game with the defensive players having control of the puck (no pass).

To make the game harder:

- Start play by having the offensive players skate 10 feet from the defensive players. Have both the offensive and defensive players skate backward, passing the puck to each other until they reach the area for a 3 v 3 game. At that point players leave the puck they have been using and wait for you to pass a new puck to begin the game.

IN REVERSE

Goal

To develop backward crossovers in a game situation.

Description

Play 2 v 2 cross-ice. Position two players on each side of the goal crease. Position a puck 10 feet from the blue line and in the middle of the ice. (See figure 8.27.)

The purpose of this game is to skate backward around a circle using backward crossovers. Each team must skate backward around the nearest faceoff circle before attempting to reach the puck. Players

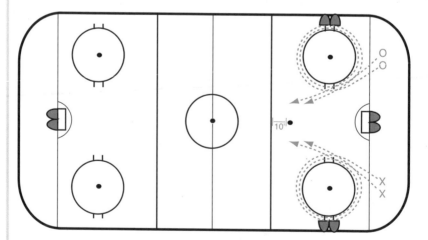

Figure 8.27   Setup for In Reverse.

must skate backward until the puck is touched. The team gaining the puck first receives two points. Once the puck is touched, a 2 v 2 game begins, with a goal counting as one point. Play continues until someone scores or the goalie holds the puck.

To make the game easier:

⊙ Allow players to pivot forward once they have completed the backward circle.

To make the game harder:

⊙ Increase the number of players to 3 v 3 or create an odd match-up such as 3 v 2 or 4 v 3. Give an additional point to the short-sided team for gaining control of the puck.

⊙ Require players to skate backward around both faceoff circles inside the blue line before retrieving the puck.

⊙ Have players skate all five circles on the ice backward, then play a 2 v 2 game at the far end of the ice.

Basic Skills

The skill work covered in this section applies to both ice and roller hockey. The primary difference is that a roller-hockey puck is usually lighter than an ice-hockey puck. All players should practice these basic skills frequently, which allows them enough time to perfect their skills.

Grip

The grip used to hold the stick is very important to players' success. To grip properly, the top hand must be at the end of the stick, just before the butt end. The lower hand should be 20 to 30 centimeters down the shaft—about shoulder length from the upper hand. To ensure that your players use the proper distance, take the elbow of the bottom arm and place it on top of the thumb of the top hand, which is holding onto the butt end of the stick. Have players rest the forearm of the bottom arm on the stick shaft, then grab the shaft with the fingers of the bottom hand. This should be the proper distance between hands. The V formed by the thumb and forefinger should point straight up the shaft (figure 8.28a and b). Players must keep the head up and use peripheral vision to look at the puck/ball. Allow younger players to look and feel for the puck/ball in the beginning.

a   b

Figure 8.28   Grip used to hold the stick.

Stationary Puck-/Ballhandling

Puck/ball handling, or dribbling, while the player is stationary may not seem to fit a hockey game scenario, but players should practice this maneuver to allow total concentration on puck-/ballhandling without concerns about skating. First, the player needs to assume the ready position. Next, with both hands on the stick and the stick blade on the rink surface, the player moves the puck/ball from side to side by rolling the wrists and shifting weight to the same skate that the puck/ball is on. This action cups the stick blade on both the forehand and backhand sides, providing better control. To roll the wrists, the player turns the forehand side of the blade downward and the backhand side upward, then reverses direction. The player handles (dribbles) the puck/ball in the middle of the blade while keeping the arms relaxed and away from the upper body (see figure 8.29a-c). Puck/ball control must be smooth, rhythmic, and quiet. Watch for players' stick blades banging on the rink surface as a sign that they are not in control of their sticks. (Check hand placement if this occurs.)

a

b

c

Figure 8.29   Stationary puck-/ballhandling.

Puck-/Ballhandling With Movement

Follow the technique described previously for stationary puck-/ballhandling, but the player must place the stick blade on a slight angle so that the puck/ball is propelled forward and to the side. Players will find comfortable angles that they wish to use.

Puck-/Ballhandling Games

KING OF THE CIRCLE

Goal

To develop creative puck-/ballhandling on the move in a confined area.

Description

This game is for three to six players, and play occurs within a faceoff circle. (See figure 8.30.)

Send players inside the circle, each with a puck/ball. The object of the game is for players to keep their pucks/balls within the circle. Encourage players to attempt to knock the pucks/balls off of the sticks of others. (This quickens the pace of the game and makes it fun.)

If players' pucks/balls leave the circle, they must skate around the outside of the circle twice before reentering the game without a puck/ball. The reentering players then try to steal pucks/balls from those skating inside the circle. However, if they steal one, then lose control of it, they must skate two laps around the circle again.

The last player with his puck/ball inside the circle wins the game.

To make the game easier:

○ Reduce the number of players.

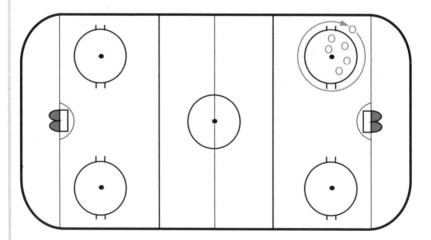

Figure 8.30 Setup for King of the Circle.

- If players' pucks/balls go out of the circle, allow them to retrieve their pucks/balls and skate around the circle twice before reentering.

To make the game harder:

- Increase the number of players.
- Give each player two pucks/balls.

FOX AND THE HOUNDS

Goal

To develop the open surface puck carry at full speed.

Description

Play this game 1 v 2 with a goalie. Position the puck carrier, or "fox," 10 feet in front of the goal line. Position the two puck chasers, or "hounds," on the goal line. (See figure 8.31.)

The object of this game is for the puck carrier to skate full speed on a breakaway toward the goal at the far end. The chasers attempt to back check and steal the puck. Allow the puck carrier a one-second head start and then "release the hounds." Give the puck carrier one point if he can reach the far blue line without being touched by the chasers and two points for a breakaway goal. If the chasers steal the puck, they receive a point. Play 1 v 2 until someone scores or the goalie holds the puck. Remember to match players by ability and skill level.

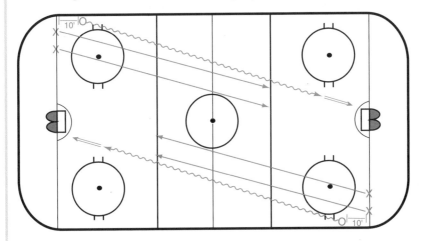

Figure 8.31 Setup for Fox and the Hounds.

(continued)

To make the game easier:

- ⊙ Start the game from the center red line.
- ⊙ Use one puck chaser, or hound.
- ⊙ Give the puck carrier, or fox, a greater lead.

To make the game harder:

- ⊙ Decrease the lead of the fox.
- ⊙ Make the game 2 v 2 and require the puck carriers to pass at least twice before shooting.

Sweep Passes

There are two types of sweep passes: forehand and backhand. The sweep pass is a normal pass that gets its name from the sweeping motion of the stick (like sweeping the floor with a broom).

Forehand Sweep Pass. The player begins in the ready position, then brings the puck/ball beyond the plane of the body (slightly behind the back skate) with the puck/ball in the middle of the stick blade (see figure 8.32a), which should be at a right angle to the target. The player keeps body weight on the back leg, head up, and eyes on the target (see figure 8.32b). Pulling with the top hand and pushing with the bottom hand, the player propels the puck/ball toward the target by sweeping the arms (see figure 8.32c). While propelling the puck/ball, the player transfers weight from the rear leg to the front leg, almost using a stepping motion (see figure 8.32d). The player's stick follows through low and toward the target, and the player immediately prepares to receive a return pass.

Backhand Sweep Pass. As in the forehand sweep pass, the player's hands remain well away from the body. The player brings the puck/ball beyond the plane of the body while shifting weight to the back leg (see figure 8.33a), keeping the head up and eyes on the target. The player cups the backhand side of the stick blade over the puck/ball. Next, the player shifts weight from the back foot to the front and sweeps the stick across the body to propel the puck/ball (see figure 8.33b). The stick follows through low, and the player immediately prepares to receive a return pass (see figure 8.33c).

Flip Pass. The flip is a situational pass used to send the puck/ball over an obstacle (e.g., an opponent's stick, body, or leg) to a target. To attempt a flip pass (or saucer pass, as it is sometimes called), the player starts with the puck/ball on the stick heel (backhand or forehand) while

Figure 8.32 Forehand sweep pass: (a) Bring the puck/ball beyond the plane of the body with the puck/ball in the middle of the stick blade; (b) keep the body weight on the back leg, head up, and eyes on the target; (c) propel the puck/ball toward the target by sweeping the arms; and (d) transfer the weight from the rear to the front leg.

he holds the stick just in front of the body. Next, the player tries to slide the puck/ball off the stick blade from the heel to the toe while following through with an upward motion. This action should cause a puck to spin and fly like a saucer in the air and cause a ball to spin like a top while flying over an obstacle toward the target.

a   b

c

Figure 8.33 Backhand sweep pass: (a) Bring the puck/ball beyond the plane of the body while shifting weight to the back leg, keeping the head up and eyes on the target; (b) shift the weight from the back foot to the front and sweep the stick across the body; and (c) follow through with the stick low and prepare to receive a return pass.

Receiving Passes

Just as important as teaching proper techniques for sending passes is helping players learn proper methods for receiving them.

Receiving Passes on the Forehand. To receive passes on the forehand, the player keeps his head up and eyes on the puck/ball carrier. The pass receiver must present a target with the stick blade, which must be in contact with the rink surface. Once the passer releases the puck/ball, the receiver's blade must remain at a 90-degree angle to the direction of the puck/ball. The player must watch the puck/ball throughout the pass reception (see figures 8.34a-c), and as the puck/ball makes contact with the stick blade, the player should provide a cushioning effect with the blade. Once the player controls the puck/ball, he should be prepared to pass. If the player provides the proper amount of cushioning, the stick blade should be in the ready position to give a pass immediately.

a

b

c

Figure 8.34 Receiving passes on the forehand.

Receiving Passes on the Backhand. To receive a pass on the backhand, players keep the head up and eyes on the passer and the puck/ball. They should follow the previously stated techniques for forehand receiving, but should substitute the backhand portion of the stick blade for the forehand portion. Finally, players need to cup the blade of the stick over the puck/ball (see figures 8.35a-c).

a

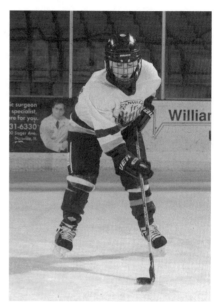

b

c

Figure 8.35 Receiving passes on the backhand.

Passing Games

MONKEY IN THE MIDDLE

Goal

To develop good decision-making skills and spacing in passing.

Description

Play this game 2 v 1. Place the two offensive players on the faceoff circle facing each other. Place the defensive player or "monkey" on the faceoff dot. (See figure 8.36.)

The object of this game is for the two offensive players to pass the puck/ball without the monkey stealing it. Offensive players are allowed to move anywhere around the faceoff circle. If a player's pass is intercepted or leaves the circle, he must go into the circle and become the monkey. For each team, keep track of how long it takes until the monkey gains control of the puck/ball or the puck/ball leaves the circle. The team that keeps the puck/ball from the monkey for the longest time period wins the game.

To make the game easier:

⊙ Play the game 3 v 1 or 4 v 1.

⊙ Allow players to move anywhere inside the circle.

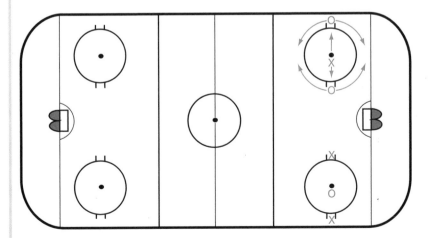

Figure 8.36 Setup for Monkey in the Middle.

(continued)

To make the game harder:

- ⊙ Increase the number of players in the game: 2 v 2, 3 v 2, 3 v 3.

- ⊙ Require all passes to be flip or backhand. A successful flip or backhand pass is worth one point for the passer.

- ⊙ Progress to a game for three players in which the passer first passes to a receiver, then attempts to block the receiver's pass to the next player. Award one point for each completed pass. Have players rotate positions.

- ⊙ Emphasize the defensive portion of this drill by rewarding players for keeping their sticks in the passing lane. For the defensive player, any steal is worth three points and any puck/ball that leaves the circle is worth one point.

- ⊙ Play 3 v 1 in the corner boards to develop the concept of the triangle offensive attack. (See figure 8.37.) Encourage players to make bump passes off the wall by rewarding a successful bump pass with a point.

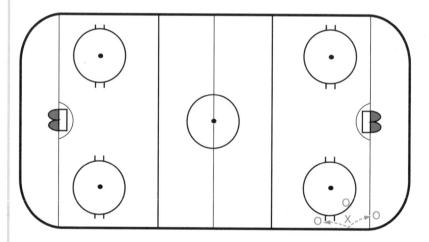

Figure 8.37 Monkey in the Middle variation playing 3 v 1.

BACKHAND BARRAGE

Goal

To develop the backhand pass and shot in a gamelike situation.

Description

Play this game 3 v 3 cross-ice. Place two nets 10 feet from the side-boards inside the blue line. Place a goaltender in each net. (See figure 8.38.)

The object of this game is to successfully complete backhand passes and backhand shots. All passes and shots must be from the backhand side. A completed backhand pass is worth one point, a backhand shot on goal one point, and a backhand goal two points. The team with the most successful backhand passes, shots, and goals wins. Do not award points for forehand shots.

To make the game easier:

⊙ Decrease the distance between the nets.

⊙ Remove the goaltenders.

To make the game harder:

⊙ Create odd-person situations such as 2 v 3 or 3 v 4.

⊙ Place a stationary player behind the goal (P) who can be used by either team as an offensive option. (See figure 8.39.)

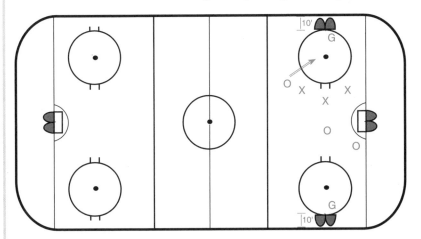

Figure 8.38   Setup for Backhand Barrage.

(continued)

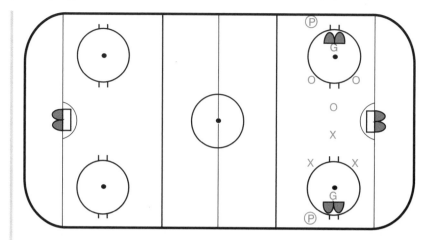

Figure 8.39 Backhand Barrage variation using a stationary player.

ONE TOUCH

Goal

To develop one-touch passing skills.

Description

Play this game 5 v 3. Begin at the center red line with five offensive players. Position two defensive players at the goal inside the offensive zone and one out on the rink. (See figure 8.40.)

The purpose of this game is to one-touch pass. (A one-touch pass involves receiving the puck/ball and immediately passing it to a teammate.) Start the game by passing the puck/ball to one of the offensive players. All five offensive players now enter the offensive zone and begin one-touch passing. In this game (1) all players must skate continuously during the game, (2) players may not carry the puck/ball at any time, and (3) all five players must touch the puck/ball at least once before the offense can attack the net. Play 5 v 3 until the defense steals the puck/ball or a goal is scored, at which time players switch roles and play a new game. Players must continue to one-touch pass during the 5 v 3 game.

Award two points for successfully completing one-touch passes to all five players. Give one point for a goal.

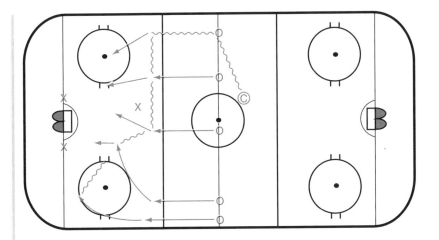

Figure 8.40   Setup for One Touch.

To make the game easier:

- ◎ Play 5 v 2.
- ◎ Introduce only one defensive player.
- ◎ Require the first set of one-touch passes to occur in the neutral zone. Once every player has touched the puck, the offense may enter the offensive zone, with all offensive players continuing to one-touch pass.

To make the game more challenging:

- ◎ Play 5 v 4.

FLIPPER

Goal

To develop the flip or aerial pass.

Description

Play this game with two offensive players and a goaltender. Create a line of sticks (with the butt end of one stick touching the blade of the next stick) from the blue line to the top line of the goal crease. (See figure 8.41.)

Teams of two pass the puck, and the passer must pass the puck over the sticks to his teammate. The team must attempt four flip passes

(continued)

over the sticks before shooting. Teams receive points based on the number of passes they make over the sticks: four points for making four passes over the sticks, three points for three passes over the sticks, and so on. Players attempt to score on the goaltender, but they are not allowed to cross over the stick barrier. Teams receive one point for a goal. The game ends when a goal is scored or the goalie holds the puck.

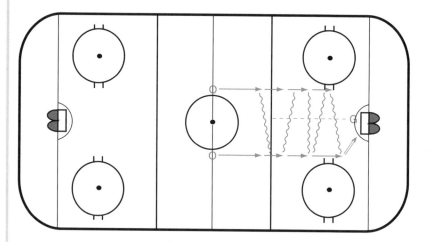

Figure 8.41　Setup for Flipper.

To make the game easier:

- Require two flip passes.
- Remove the goaltender.

To make the game harder:

- Raise the height of the barrier (for example, use small cones).
- Make two lines of sticks and have three offensive players, requiring each player to touch and make a flip pass (see figure 8.42).
- Add a defensive player in front of the net.
- Position a stationary passer in the corner behind the goal line. The stationary passer can be used as an extra attack option (play 3 v 1).
- Use a line of defensive players as the barrier between passers. (Caution: This activity should be performed only by advanced players. In this situation players may be hit by flying pucks.)

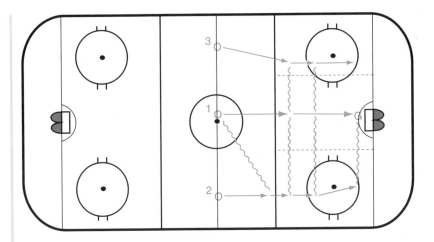

Figure 8.42   Flipper variation with three offensive players.

Open Surface Carry

A player uses this maneuver in open surface when he will not be challenged by opponents. The player needs to control the stick with the top hand only and push the puck/ball slightly ahead with the bottom edge of the stick blade by straightening the arm at the elbow, making sure he keeps the puck/ball in contact with the stick blade. It is important for the hand controlling the stick to be on top of the stick, away from the upper body. You can practice this maneuver on both forehand and backhand sides and use full-rink surface carries or one-on-zero games.

Shooting

Because scoring goals is the basic offensive objective of hockey, shooting is one of the most-practiced maneuvers in the game. Players must understand these important concepts:

1. No matter which shot players take, proper form is extremely important.
2. Accuracy is the second most important factor in shooting.
3. Quickness is a kind of secret weapon (if everyone—especially the goalkeeper—has time to prepare, effectiveness is lost).
4. Shot variety makes a difference (if players take the same shot every time, they lose the element of surprise).

We have intentionally omitted the slapshot from this book because of its inaccuracy, the length of time required to take the shot, and the inability of most young players to produce the lower- and upper-body strength necessary to master it.

Forehand Sweep (Wrist) Shot. The player should use the same basic grip as in passing, bringing the puck/ball beyond the plane of the body and keeping it in contact with the stick blade until he is ready to release it. The player then shifts weight to the back foot. While sweeping the puck/ball forward, he transfers weight to the front foot (see figure 8.43a). The player's head must be up with eyes on the target (see figure 8.43b). To release the puck/ball, the player snaps and rolls the wrists, pulling the top hand and pushing the bottom hand. Next, he follows through low for a low shot and high for a high shot. The player keeps his wrists cocked until the moment of release and then snaps them through the shot (see figure 8.43c).

a

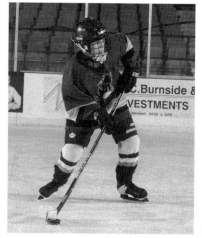

b

c

Figure 8.43 Forehand sweep (wrist) shot: (a) Transfer weight forward; (b) keep the head up, with the eyes on the target; and (c) snap and roll the wrists, pulling with the bottom hand and pushing with the top hand.

Backhand Sweep Shot. The backhand sweep shot is the same as the wrist shot, only it is taken from the backhand position. It is extremely important that the player keep the knee bent and get most of his power by transferring weight to the opposite foot.

Flip Shot. Think of a flip shot as a clearing shot or pass. It is mainly used to relieve pressure in the defensive end by throwing or flipping the puck/ball out of the zone. The primary focus should be on lofting the puck/ball over any opponents and out of the zone, not on speed or accuracy. To practice this maneuver, the player should place the hands in the proper position on the stick shaft, open—not cup—the forehand portion of the stick blade, and attempt to lift the puck/ball using a quick, sharp upward movement of the open-faced blade.

Snapshot. Think of this shot as a wrist shot with a little extra snap at the end. The player uses the same techniques as the wrist shot, but just before releasing the puck/ball, he should forcefully snap through the puck/ball. The player needs to strike the rink surface one to two inches behind the puck/ball. Hand position, follow-through, upper-body position, and weight transfer remain the same as in the wrist shot.

Error Detection and Correction for Shooting

ERROR   Improper weight transfer causing a weak or inaccurate shot

CORRECTION   Place the weight on the back foot, stepping through to the front foot while shooting.

ERROR   Improper hand positioning

CORRECTION   Hands should be shoulder-width apart.

ERROR   Hands too close to upper body, causing improper wrist action

CORRECTION   Hands need to have room to flow. Hands and arms need to be out comfortably away from the chest and waist.

Shooting Games

FIVE PRIME SHOOTING

Goal

To develop shooting accuracy on the five prime scoring areas of the net.

Description

Play this 2 v 1 game cross-rink (see figure 8.44). Place a net 15 feet from the sideboards on each side of the rink. Place a "shooter tutor" in each net, which is a tarp with a goalie painted on the front and the five holes cut out are attached to the netting with bungee cords. This shooter tutor clearly defines the five prime scoring areas: bottom left, top left, top right, bottom right, and five-hole (six inches above the ground in the center). This will help the shooter look past the goaltender and find the open net. (A goaltender can substitute for the shooter tutor, but he must stand still during the game.) Run two or three games concurrently.

The object of the game is to attempt to hit the five prime scoring areas of the net. Hitting one of the five areas earns two points for the shooter's team. The team registering the most points wins the game. Play for no more than two minutes and change players by having the players leave the rink on the whistle. Dump the puck/ball to start the next game.

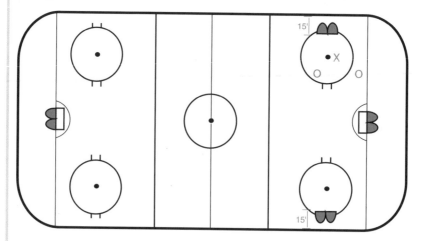

Figure 8.44 Setup for Five Prime Shooting.

To make the game easier:

⊙ Play 3 v 1.

To make the game more challenging:

⊙ Play 2 v 2 or 3 v 3.

⊙ Decrease the distance of the nets from the boards.

⊙ Add a passer from behind the goal line (P) who puts a puck/ball in play immediately after a successful shot. This player is also an extra attack option but must stand stationary. (See figure 8.45.)

⊙ Require that shots be one-timers off the pass.

⊙ Designate one of the five scoring areas as a bonus shot: hitting that area gives the player three points.

⊙ Designate a particular shot worth three points: wrist shot, snap-shot, or backhand.

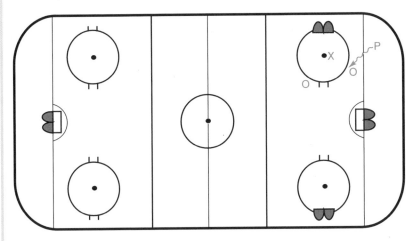

Figure 8.45   Five Prime Shooting variation with an additional passer.

COACHES' CHOICE

Goal

To develop different shooting techniques in a game situation.

Description

Play cross-rink 3 v 3 with two goals 10 feet from the sideboards. (See figure 8.46.)

(continued)

The object of the game is to emphasize a particular shot by giving it bonus points. Begin the game 3 v 3 with two goalies. Announce that wrist shots on net are worth one point and wrist shot goals are worth two points. All other goals are not counted. In later games, reward backhand or snapshots.

To make the game easier:

○ Play 3 v 2 or 4 v 3.

To make the game harder:

○ Play 3 v 3 with an additional player designated as the shooter. (See figure 8.47.) The shooter stands halfway between the nets

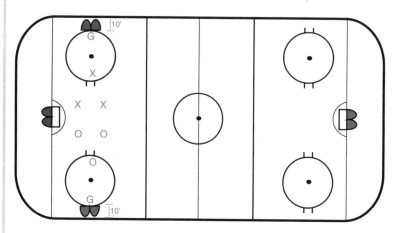

Figure 8.46 Setup for Coaches' Choice.

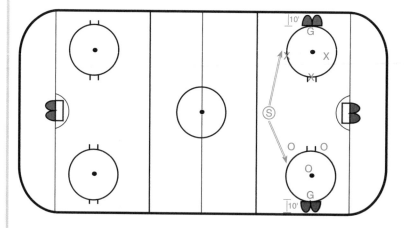

Figure 8.47 Coaches' Choice variation with an additional shooter.

and shoots on goal for the team on offense. Require that the first shot come from the shooter and that he not be guarded. Give two points for a tipped shot for a goal and one point for a rebound goal. All other goals are not counted. Rotate players so that all get a chance to be the shooter.

Checking Techniques

Because of the lack of body checking in roller hockey and in the lower age levels of ice hockey, this discussion focuses on stick checking.

Stick Checking. This maneuver requires a player to use the stick blade to poke or strike an opponent's stick blade or a puck/ball in an opponent's possession. The stick check is generally executed with one hand—usually the top hand—on the stick shaft. To execute the stick check, the player quickly extends the arm with the stick toward the puck/ball. The player must not lunge at the puck/ball, and he must remain in the proper skating position. The stick blade must remain on the rink surface to make contact with the puck/ball.

Lifting the Opponent's Stick. A player uses this stick check when coming up behind an opponent who is carrying the puck/ball. With an element of surprise, the player slides the stick under the opponent's stick and lifts quickly (see figures 8.48a-b). The player must bring the stick back to the rink surface quickly to recover the puck/ball (see figure 8.48c). The player should immediately skate away from the opposing player.

Covering the Opponent. Players execute this technique differently, depending on whether the opponent has the puck/ball. If the opponent does not have the puck/ball, players should keep themselves between the opponent and the puck/ball, staying within one stick length of the opponent to cover that player effectively. If the opposing player has the puck/ball, then players should try to force the opposition to the outside portions of the rink where the puck/ball carrier will eventually run out of skating room. Once players get within a comfortable distance, they should do one of the stick-checking maneuvers mentioned previously. Remind players not to lunge after the puck/ball.

Figure 8.48 Lifting the opponent's stick: (a and b) Slide the stick under the opponent's stick and lift quickly; and (c) recover the puck/ball.

Checking Games

THE LONG SKATE

Goal

To develop stick-checking skills.

Description

Play this game with three offensive and three defensive players. Set up eight cones between the blue line and the goal line (see figure 8.49).

The purpose of this game is for the defensive players to use a specific stick-checking action to steal the puck from an offensive player. Place one defensive player and one offensive player in each of the three zones. In zone A, the goal of the defensive player is to poke check the puck off the offensive player. In zone B, the goal of the defensive player is to lift the stick and steal the puck. In zone C, the goal of the defensive player is to press the stick of the offensive player and steal the puck. Whoever has the puck at the end of each zone passes it to the next offensive player.

If a defensive player successfully uses the designated checking skill, he receives two points. An offensive player receives two points if he

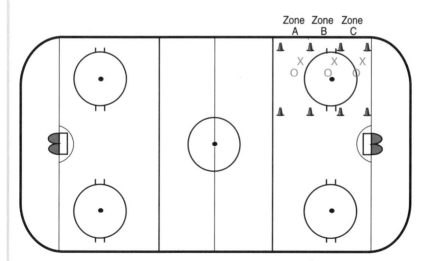

Figure 8.49   Setup for The Long Skate.

(continued)

can move through the zone without losing possession of the puck. After players have played through the zones twice, have both players in zone A rotate to zone B, zone B to zone C, and zone C to zone A. Once players have rotated through all three zones, have offensive players and defensive players switch roles.

To make the game easier:

- ⊙ Allow players to use any of the stick-checking skills.
- ⊙ Award one point for doing the stick check correctly.

To make the game harder:

- ⊙ Create a 2 v 2 situation in each zone by positioning two defensive players in each zone against the two offensive players.

TIGHT CHECKING

Goal

To develop checking skills.

Description

Play this game 2 v 2. Set up a 20 x 40-foot area using four cones, and designate an end line for the defensive team to defend. (See figure 8.50.)

The goal is for the defenders to stay between the offense and the end line. The defense earns points in this game by not allowing the

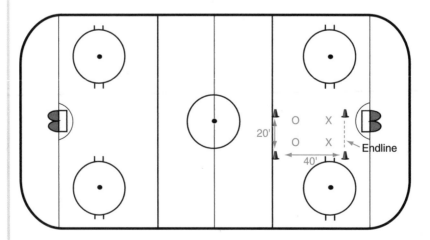

Figure 8.50   Setup for Tight Checking.

offense to advance the puck/ball by passing or carrying it behind them (one point). Give two points for creating a turnover. After creating a turnover, the defense gives the puck/ball back to the offense. Switch roles after three minutes.

To make the game easier:

- Play 2 v 3.
- Decrease the width between the cones.

To make the game harder:

- Play 3 v 2 or 4 v 2.
- Increase the width between the cones to give the offense more room.
- Decrease the distance between end lines.

NO MAN'S LAND

Goal

To develop legal body-checking skills.

Description

Play 2 v 2 along the sideboard. Set a goal at the goal line and the other goal at the blue line. Place a line of cones 20 feet from the wall to delineate the fourth boundary. (See figure 8.51.)

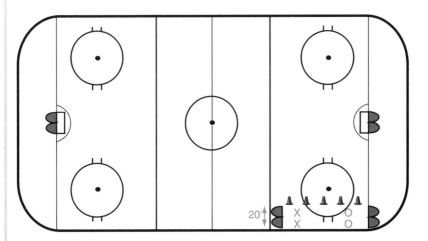

Figure 8.51   Setup for No Man's Land.

(continued)

The purpose of this game is to apply legal body checks in a 2 v 2 game along the boards. Award two points for each legal check and deduct two points for each illegal check. Give one point for a goal. Play for 90 seconds, then send in two new teams. Note that it is important to match opponents by size and skill when doing a contact drill.

To make the game easier:

⊙ Decrease the width of the playing area.

To make the game harder:

⊙ Play 3 v 3.

⊙ Play without sticks and require teams to kick the puck into an empty net.

Goaltending

Goalkeeper is the position that coaches most frequently neglect when developing players' skills. Coaches must spend time with goalies to help them attain and improve on the basic skills they need to succeed.

Differences Between Ice Hockey and Roller Hockey Goaltending

The biggest difference between ice hockey and roller hockey goaltending is that ice hockey goalkeepers can actually slide their skates across the ice to move laterally. The blades are sharpened with a very small hollow specifically for this purpose. Roller hockey goalies must pick up their skates to move laterally, creating a second when they are vulnerable to being scored on. To minimize this risk, goalkeepers need to master the T-push maneuver. Another big difference between the two sports is that ice hockey goalies can execute a two-pad slide with some ease. In roller hockey, depending on the surface, goalkeepers may need to apply more force to move the same distance.

Stance

Goalkeepers must start in the ready position; otherwise, the moves they must master become more difficult to perform. The ready position begins with weight on the middle of the skates to the heels, legs shoulder-width apart, knees bent, rear down, shoulders back, stick in front of and between the skates, gloves off the pads and in front of the body, and catch glove above the hip (see figure 8.52).

Figure 8.52 Goaltender stance.

Movement

You must teach lateral movement to goalkeepers so that they can cover the entire net without leaving a large shooting space for the opposition. Break the movement down into short and long distances. The shuffle step is good for short-distance lateral movements, and the T-push is good for long-distance lateral movements.

Shuffle Step. To execute the shuffle step, the goalkeeper remains in ready position while shuffling the feet with small steps either right or left. The goalie should keep the shoulders square and the back to the net.

T-Push. To use the T-push, the goalkeeper turns the lead foot in the direction he wishes to go and pushes off with the inside edge of the other foot. Once the goalie reaches the desired location or distance, he stops and assumes the ready position.

Telescoping. Telescoping is the goalkeepers' art of forward and backward movement. The goalie moves forward by pushing off the inside edge of one foot to obtain power, and then gliding in the ready position to the desired position or distance. To move backward, the goalkeeper uses the inside edge of one foot to draw the letter C on the rink surface and then glides in the ready position to the desired position or distance.

Error Detection and Correction for Goalkeeper Ready Position

ERROR   Pads too far apart and goalies too much on the inside skate edges

CORRECTION   Correct the V-position of skates and pads. Stay on middle edges of blades/wheels.

ERROR   Elbow of catch glove too tight to body

CORRECTION   Keep five hole (hole between pads) small. Move elbow away from body.

ERROR   Gloves resting on pads, creating overlapping coverage

CORRECTION   Move gloves away from body (to the side).

ERROR   Shoulder too far forward

CORRECTION   Keep weight over the middle of the skates (balls of the feet).

Goaltending Movement Games

AROUND THE WORLD

Goal

To develop a goaltender's ability to telescope and properly play the angle of the shot.

Description

Position shooters in an umbrella formation starting at the faceoff dot and ending at the opposite faceoff dot. Give each shooter several pucks/balls. Place one goaltender in the goal and another behind the goal. (See figure 8.53.)

The purpose of this game is for the goaltender to make saves from different angles. Starting at the right faceoff dot, each player shoots a puck/ball, one at a time. Have shooters count to one after the goalie

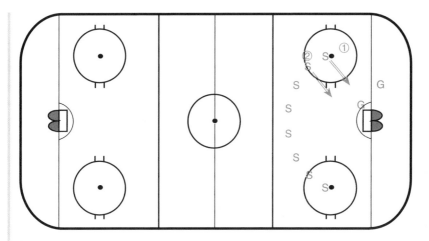

Figure 8.53 Setup for Around the World.

touches the puck/ball or it goes in the net before shooting the next one. This will give the goalie a chance to prepare.

If the goaltender makes the save, he continues on to the next shot. If the puck goes in the net, the goalie leaves the net and allows the second goaltender to enter the game. The game begins again at the right faceoff dot and continues until someone scores on the goalie. Goaltenders alternate until one makes a save on each shooter and wins the game. After the first round, goalies start by receiving a shot from where they were scored on the last time.

To make the game easier:

- Increase the distance of the shooters from the net.
- Increase the amount of time (count to two) between shots, allowing the goaltender to reposition.
- Allow goalies the option of taking a second shot from a shooter. If a goal is scored again, the goalie must go back to the beginning of the game.

To make the game harder:

- Decrease the distance of the shooters from the net.
- Decrease the amount of time between shots. Tell shooters to shoot immediately after a goalie touches the previous shot or it goes in the net.

REBOUND

Goal

To develop the goaltending skills of freezing the puck/ball and stopping rebounds.

Description

Position two shooters 15 feet from the net and two rebounders to the left and right of the goaltender. (See figure 8.54.)

The purpose of this game is for the goaltender to stop a shot and attempt to hold the puck/ball. Start the game by having the right shooter shoot. Once the shot has been taken, the two rebounders go after the rebound and attempt to score. Play stops when the goalie freezes the puck/ball or a goal is scored. Alternate which shooter starts the play. Give two points to the goalie for saving and holding the initial shot and one point for freezing the puck/ball off a rebound; give one point to the shooters for a goal scored. Play to 10 points.

To make the game easier:

⊙ Use only one shooter and one rebounder.

To make the game harder:

⊙ Give a puck/ball to the rebounders. If the goalie freezes the initial shot or the puck goes in the net, continue play by having the rebounder attempt to score with another puck/ball.

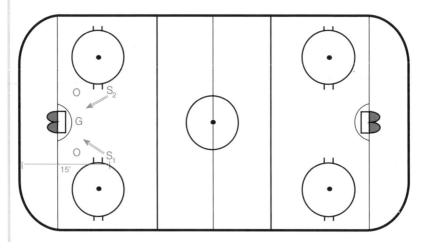

Figure 8.54 Setup for Rebound.

- Force the goaltender to play without his stick.
- Require the goaltender to lie on his side to make saves.
- Make this a screen-and-deflection game by having the rebounders stand in front of the goalie. Position the shooters 30 feet from the net and tell them to shoot low, medium-paced shots. Score the same as previously.

HANG ON!

Goal

For the goaltender to develop movement in a game situation.

Description

Position two shooters 25 feet from the net and 15 feet apart. (See figure 8.55.)

The purpose of this game is for the goaltender to move quickly and get in position for a shot. Have the shooters pass to each other a predetermined number of times (the goalie should not be aware of the number of passes). The number should not be more than four in order to better simulate game situations. Give one point to the goalie for each save and one point to the shooters for each goal.

To make the game easier:

- Increase the distance of the shooters from the net.
- Announce the number of passes to be made.

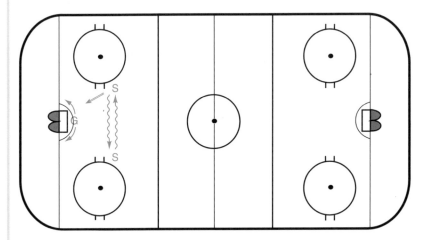

Figure 8.55   Setup for Hang On!

(continued)

To make the game more challenging:

⊙ Make this a 2 v 1, 3 v 1, or 3 v 2 game, starting in the neutral zone (figure 8.56).

3 v. 1   3 v. 2

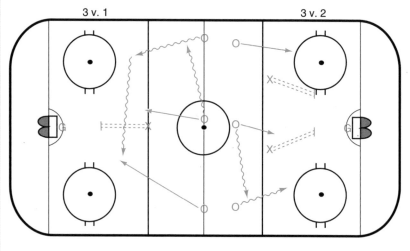

Figure 8.56   Hang On! variation playing 3 v 1 and 3 v 2.

Common Save Techniques

Now that the players can balance in the ready position and move around the crease, they need to know how to use the equipment they wear to stop the puck/ball.

Stick Saves. Using a firm grip, the goalkeeper holds the stick in the blocker glove hand, just above the paddle (widened portion of the goal stick) on the shaft. The most important part of the stick save is that the blade of the stick must remain on the rink surface at all times to stop the low shot; the blade should not rest on the front of the skates. A stick save made on low shots should angle shots away from the front of the net, toward the corners. The stick should cushion shots aimed right at the goalkeeper. During high shots the goalie uses the stick like a baseball bat, directing the stick paddle to the puck/ball. Remind the goalkeeper to direct the puck/ball away from the goal mouth.

Poke Checks. A poke check is a sudden move that the goalkeeper makes with the stick to contact the puck/ball with the stick blade. There are three basic types of poke checks: standing, power, and diving. The goalie makes the standing poke check by thrusting the stick out toward the puck/ball, almost like throwing the stick at the puck/ball, without letting go of the shaft. The goal stick must have a large butt end or a wad

Error Detection and Correction for Stick Saves

ERROR   Raising the stick blade off the rink surface

CORRECTION   Force the stick down to the surface. Allow the hand to slide up and down the shaft of the stick.

ERROR   Failing to keep a buffer between the stick blade and the skates

CORRECTION   Keep at least six inches between the blade of the stick and the toes of the skates.

ERROR   Failing to clear pucks/balls away from the goal mouth

CORRECTION   Angle the stick to the side slightly so that the puck/ball is directed at the corners.

of tape on the end of the shaft to stop the stick from sliding out of the hand. After thrusting the stick at the puck/ball, the goalkeeper draws the stick back quickly and assumes the ready position. The other two poke checks are similar in execution but are started in different body positions. The power poke check is executed with the stick-side knee down. For a diving poke check the goalie thrusts the stick at the puck/ball, then follows with the body. Once the body starts to slide on the rink surface, the goalkeeper must cover all the surface possible, so he spreads the legs in a large V, pointing the toes toward the direction he is sliding.

Skate Saves. Skate saves are broken down into two different types: standing and one-knee skate saves. If a goalie can reach the puck/ball with a standing skate save, he can also reach it with the stick. Because he should attempt the stick save first, the goalkeeper should use the standing skate save only as a backup to the stick save. To execute this save properly, the goalkeeper should point the toe of the skate he wishes to move toward the puck/ball and push off the inside edge of the opposite skate, causing the turned foot to roll or glide across the rink surface. The stick must be in front of the skate pointed toward the puck/ball when the goalkeeper tries to make the save.

The goalkeeper executes the one-knee skate save while resting on the inside knee. He must place all weight on the inside knee, keep the skate wheels or blade on the rink surface, snap the leg out, keep the stick down and glove up, and try not to fall backward. The goalkeeper should avoid using the gloves to push himself up.

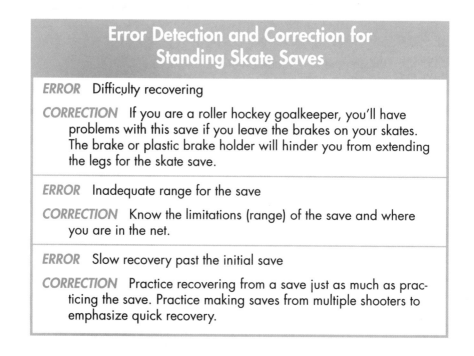

Error Detection and Correction for Standing Skate Saves

ERROR   Difficulty recovering

CORRECTION   If you are a roller hockey goalkeeper, you'll have problems with this save if you leave the brakes on your skates. The brake or plastic brake holder will hinder you from extending the legs for the skate save.

ERROR   Inadequate range for the save

CORRECTION   Know the limitations (range) of the save and where you are in the net.

ERROR   Slow recovery past the initial save

CORRECTION   Practice recovering from a save just as much as practicing the save. Practice making saves from multiple shooters to emphasize quick recovery.

Error Detection and Correction for One-Knee Skate Saves

ERROR   First movement is up with the shoulders

CORRECTION   Begin in the ready position, then drop down on the inside knee, keeping the upper body still.

ERROR   Leaning away from the shot (not covering the net with the upper body)

CORRECTION   Keep the upper body straight and upright while keeping the shoulders square to the puck/ball.

ERROR   Sitting back on the inside skate

CORRECTION   Rest on the knee.

ERROR   No snap to the extended leg

CORRECTION   Quickly extend the leg, making the save with a snap, and recover quickly.

Butterfly Pad Save. Goalies use this save when there is a large amount of traffic in front of the net or against a deking forward. Advantages over the skate save are that goalkeepers can cover more area and they have better chances of guessing correctly. One of the greatest disadvantages of this save is that while using the pads, goalies give up more rebounds in front of the net.

The most important aspect of the butterfly is covering the upper portion of the net with the goalkeeper's upper body. To perform this save properly, the goalie drops to the knees while pointing the toes out, creating a V. The goal is to cover as much rink surface as possible with this V while keeping the upper body in the ready position (see figure 8.57).

There is also a half-butterfly variation of this save performed by dropping one knee instead of both.

Two-Pad Slide Save. The best way to describe this save is to think of a foot-first slide into second base in baseball. To perform this save, the goalkeeper must turn his skates into a T, push off with the foot farthest from the side he intends to slide toward, and glide with the other. Next, he drops the knee while kicking out the skates and slides across on the hip with the pads stacked on top of each other (see figure 8.58a and b). Goalies use this save on a quick play around the net or on a breakaway.

Figure 8.57 Butterfly pad save.

Error Detection and Correction for Butterfly Pad Saves

ERROR　Weight not on knees

CORRECTION　Keep the weight on the knees with the upper body upright.

ERROR　Improper pad placement

CORRECTION　Keep pads flat on the surface by driving the knees down.

ERROR　Improper stick placement

CORRECTION　Cover the opening between the legs with the stick. The stick should not be angled, but straight up and down. As always, keep the stick about three to six inches in front of the pads.

a

b

Figure 8.58　Two-pad slide save.

Glove Saves. Goalkeepers can use the pads and gloves to protect the upper portion of the net rather well if they stay in the ready position. Overall, goalies will be more comfortable with the gloves than the pads, and they usually favor the catching glove over the blocker, which is worn on the hand holding the stick.

The goalkeeper uses the catch glove as if it were a baseball glove, following the puck/ball into the glove and squeezing firmly (see figure 8.59). The biggest mistake the inexperienced goalie makes is trying to catch too much. He comes across the body with the catch glove, which brings him out of the ready position. The goaltender also tries to catch everything down by the feet, which brings him even farther out of the ready position and puts the head down. Remind the goalkeeper always to follow the puck/ball into the glove.

It takes a little more time to use the blocker proficiently, but if the goalkeeper thinks of it as an extension of the stick, he may master proper technique easily. The goalie should follow the puck/ball into the blocker and direct it into a corner away from the net. He should not swipe at the puck/ball. The goalkeeper should also be aware of the angle at which the blocker hits the puck/ball. If the angle is too great, the puck/ball will pop up into the air. The goalie should learn to trap on the blocker with the catch glove by placing the catch glove on top of the blocker once the blocker makes contact with the puck/ball.

Figure 8.59   Glove save.

Error Detection and Correction for Glove Saves

ERROR   Pulling up out of fear

CORRECTION   Use soft tennis balls or rolled-up socks and graduate to pucks/balls once confidence becomes greater.

ERROR   Inadequate lateral movement into the shot

CORRECTION   Practice T-push or side-step maneuvers.

ERROR   Giving rebounds out in front of the net off stick glove

CORRECTION   Snap the wrist and angle the blocker to the corners.

ERROR   Coming across the body with opposite side glove

CORRECTION   Do not cross the midline of the body with any glove.

ERROR   Taking eyes off the puck/ball

CORRECTION   Concentrate on the puck/ball and not the shooter.

Playing the Angles. The most important skill for the goalkeeper to learn is the art of playing the angles: cutting down on the amount of net the shooter sees behind the goalie. The goalkeeper's best strategy is to avoid sitting back in the net. On a regular shot the goalie must come out, stay square to the shooter, and play the puck/ball, not the shooter. If the puck/ball is out in front of the net, the goalkeeper may come out, but if the puck/ball is to the side or behind the net, he must stay in the net.

Breakaway Saves. The key to effective defense against breakaways is timing. Teach goalkeepers these basic steps for mastering breakaways: (a) come out extra far, (b) back up with the shooter no deeper than the top of the crease, and (c) make the save (possibly with a two-pad slide). Try not to make the first move. Goalkeepers must learn to time their backward movements and to react to the shooters.

Screen Shot Saves. Teach goalkeepers to defend screen shots by getting low and fighting the screen persistently. The ideal save is the butterfly.

The best way to practice defending against screen shots is to use a screen-shot board. You can make one with a sheet and some framing boards. Design the board so that a puck/ball shot under the sheet on one side cannot be seen by goalies on the other side until the last minute.

Save Technique Game

ON THE HOT SPOT

Goal

For the goaltender to develop common save techniques.

Description

Play this game cross-rink 2 v 2 with two goaltenders. Position the nets 10 feet from the sideboards. (See figure 8.60.)

The purpose of this game is to practice certain save techniques. Choose a particular technique (e.g., stick save, glove save, butterfly pad save) that the goaltender should use to stop the puck/ball. Before the game begins, emphasize to the players that they should shoot in an area that will force the goalie to make the predetermined save. Play for five minutes.

Give the goaltender two points for each save performed using the predetermined save. Do not award points for the use of other save techniques. Give the goaltender who allows the fewest number of goals an additional two points. The goaltender with the most points wins. Continue the game using other save techniques.

To make the game easier:

◎ Play the game 2 v 3.

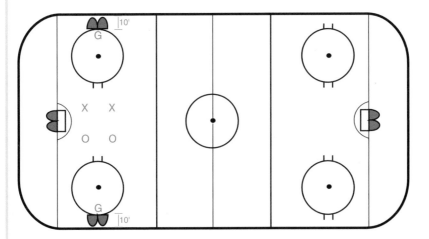

Figure 8.60 Setup for On The Hot Spot.

(continued)

To make the game harder:

- ⊙ Add a stationary shooter in front of each net who can screen the goaltender and play for rebounds.
- ⊙ Require the goaltender to begin the game lying on his or her side.

Deflections. If a goalkeeper thinks that a deflection is possible, he must move toward the deflection without losing the angle of the initial shot, then turn and square off to the deflection.

Covering Up the Puck/Ball—Hunger. When a puck/ball is loose in front of the net, the goalie must react quickly to "pounce" on it (cover it up). The analogy of a hungry tiger pouncing on a piece of meat illustrates this save technique.

Error Detection and Correction for Covering Up the Puck/Ball

ERROR   Failing to keep the head up

CORRECTION   Keep the head up at all times.

ERROR   Using the stick for protection

CORRECTION   Cover the puck/ball with the catch glove only. Place the stick and blocker in front of the catch glove once the puck/ball is covered to protect the glove hand from the players' sticks.

Puck/Ball Behind the Net Saves. Teach goalkeepers to use this procedure when the puck/ball goes behind the net. First, as shooters move behind the net, the goalie should move to the side post closest to the shooter, remain square, and turn the head in the direction of the shooter. Once the shooter reaches the middle of the back of the net (the safest spot), the goalie must quickly move across the net (T-push) and cover the other side post. The goalie must be ready for a quick pass from behind the net and a wraparound shot.

Two-On-One and Three-On-Two Saves. On an odd-player rush (two-on-one or three-on-two), the goalie's main responsibility is the shooter. If a late pass is made to the open player, the two-pad slide is usually the save of choice. Any player coming out of the corner provides the toughest play that a goalkeeper has to handle.

The goalkeeper needs to know his limits and simplify decisions by making a mark on the rink surface at his maximum poke-checking point. When poke checking, the goalkeeper should neither go down nor lunge the shoulders forward; doing so sacrifices lateral mobility.

As shooters approach, the goalkeeper should come out at them (not leaving the post too early), force them to take as much time as possible, and move them into defenders. The wider a shooter goes, the better. Remind the goalkeeper that players on their forehand move across the net more easily and have more angle, but they are also more vulnerable to a poke check because the puck/ball is out in front. Also remind the goalkeeper that players on their backhand can shield the puck/ball better and are less vulnerable to a poke check. Teach goalies that a fake poke check often forces a player away from the net.

In a two-on-one a goalkeeper's job is to take away the short side, and in a two-on-one out of the corner, players will often pass rather than carry the puck/ball out. Goalkeepers should not allow those passes to come through their reach limits!

Faceoff. If a shooter is on his forehand, the goalkeeper should line up with the faceoff. But if the shooter is on his backhand, the goalie should either line up with gunners or know where gunners are and be able to get there.

General Rules (Easy Angle Rule)

- ◎ Face the puck/ball and shooters.

- ◎ Line up so that the puck/ball hits you in the middle of the chest, with shoulders square to the puck/ball, requiring you to move only half of the body to make any save.

- ◎ Position yourself in the middle of the shooters' line-of-sight angles and move out to the top of the crease, taking away the net that shooters can see. Get set and avoid moving too far.

- ◎ Make yourself look big, avoid covering up equipment that is covering a piece of the net, and always try to cover an open piece of the net.

- ◎ Point skates at shooters and try to move a half step behind the puck/ball.

- ◎ Make opponents shoot to the side of the net that you (the goalkeeper) are approaching, not the side you are leaving.

- ◎ Control the puck/ball and control play so that you know where opponents are. You should play the four segments of the net and read shooters on all plays, including breakaways.

Goalkeepers should learn these maneuvers at a slow pace, then progress to a more rapid pace as their skills improve. Teach them that technique is more important than quickness in the beginning.

If you are lucky enough to have two goalies, use the second goalie as you would use a video camera. Being able to see the open areas and the amount of net available will help him when it is his turn at goalie. Remember, the day is over when the overweight player who couldn't skate plays goalie. Work with your goalies every chance you get. The entire team will benefit from it!

Season Plans

Hopefully you've learned a lot from this book: what your responsibilities as a coach are, how to communicate well and provide for safety, how to use the games approach to teach and shape skills, and how to coach on game days. But game days make up only a portion of your season—you and your players will spend more time in practice than in competition. How well you conduct practices and prepare your players for competition will greatly affect both you and your players' enjoyment and success throughout the season.

In this chapter, then, we present three season plans: one for 8- to 9-year-olds, one for 10- to 11-year-olds, and one for 12- to 14-year-olds. Use these plans as guidelines for conducting your practices. These plans are not the only way to approach your season, but they do present an appropriate teaching progression. Remember to incorporate the games approach as you use these plans, using Game 1 to put your players in a game-like situation that introduces them to the main tactic or skill that you want them to learn that day. Then guide your players through a short question-and-answer session that leads to the skill practice. Here you should conduct one or two skill practices in which you will teach players the tactic or skill and then conduct a fun drill for them to practice that skill.

Refer to chapter 5 (page 39) for how to run a practice. In chapter 8 you will find descriptions of all the tactics and skills, and games you can use to practice them. Throughout the season plans we refer you to the appropriate pages for those tactics and skills and games.

Remember to keep the introductions, demonstrations, and explanations of the tactics and skills brief. As the players practice, attend to individual players, guiding them with tips or with further demonstration.

Good luck and good coaching!

Hockey Season Plan for 8- to 9-Year-Olds

Many 8- to 9-year-olds have had little or no exposure to hockey. Don't assume they have any knowledge of the game. Help them explore the basic tactics and skills of the sport, as suggested in the following season plan.

Practice 1

- **Purpose:** Intro to the game and the team
- **Warm-up**
- **Game 1:** One-Foot Faceoff (see page 121)
- **Skill Development of skating with stick**
- **Game 2:** One-Foot Faceoff (see page 121)
- **Cool-down and Review**

Practice 2

- **Purpose:** Intro to the game
- **Warm-up**
- **Game 1:** Freeze Tag (see page 119)
- **Skill Development of skating and stopping**

- **Game 2:** Freeze Tag (see page 119)
- **Cool-down and Review**

Practice 3

- **Purpose:** Puckhandling
- **Warm-up**
- **Game 1:** King of the Circle (see page 142)
- **Skill Development of basic puckhandling**
- **Game 2:** King of the Circle (see page 142)
- **Cool-down and Review**

Practice 4

- **Purpose:** Learn skating edges
- **Warm-up**
- **Game 1:** Stop and Go (see page 126)
- **Introduce receiving serve game**
- **Game 2:** Stop and Go (see page 126)
- **Cool-down and Review**

Practice 5

- **Purpose:** Forehand Shooting
- **Warm-up**
- **Game 1:** Five Prime Shooting (see page 158)
- **Skill Development for forehand shooting**
- **Game 2:** Five Prime Shooting (see page 158)
- **Cool-down and Review**

Practice 6

- **Purpose:** Passing
- **Warm-up**
- **Game 1:** Monkey in the Middle (see page 149)
- **Skill development of passing**
- **Game 2:** Monkey in the Middle (see page 149)
- **Cool-down and Review**

Practice 7

- **Purpose:** Backward skating
- **Warm-up**
- **Game 1:** Backward Blitz (see page 137)
- **Skill Development for skating backward**
- **Game 2:** Backward Blitz (see page 137)
- **Cool-down and Review**

Practice 8

- **Purpose:** Puckhandling
- **Warm-up**
- **Game 1:** Fox and the Hounds (see page 143)
- **Skill Development for puckhandling in open spaces**
- **Game 2:** Fox and the Hounds (see page 143)
- **Cool-down and Review**

Practice 9

- **Purpose:** Backhand passing and shooting
- **Warm-up**
- **Game 1:** Backhand Barrage (see page 151)
- **Skill Development for backhand passing and shooting**
- **Game 2:** Backhand Barrage (see page 151)
- **Cool-down and Review**

Practice 10

- **Purpose:** Flip shot and pass
- **Warm-up**
- **Game 1:** Flipper (see page 153)
- **Skill Development for flip shot and passing**
- **Game 2:** Flipper (see page 153)
- **Cool-down and Review**

Practice 11

- **Purpose:** Offensive triangle
- **Warm-up**

- **Game 1:** Backhand Barrage (see page 151)
- **Skill review for offensive triangle**
- **Game 2:** Backhand Barrage (see page 151)
- **Cool-down and Review**

Practice 12

- **Purpose:** Basic checking
- **Warm-up**
- **Game 1:** The Long Skate (see page 163)
- **Skill Development for stick checking**
- **Game 2:** The Long Skate (see page 163)
- **Cool-down and Review**

Practice 13

- **Purpose:** Effective team offense
- **Warm-up**
- **Game 1:** One Touch (see page 152)
- **Skill Development for Team Offense**
- **Game 2:** One Touch (see page 152)
- **Cool-down and Review**

Practice 14

- **Purpose:** Team defense
- **Warm-up**
- **Game 1:** Coaches' Choice (see page 159)
- **Skill Development for Team Defense**
- **Game:** Scrimmage
- **Cool-down and Review**

Hockey Season Plan for 10- to 11-Year-Olds

This season plan builds upon the previous one as players practice the fundamental tactics and skills and add a few new tactics, including power skating, flip passing, and checking.

Practice 1

- **Purpose:** Intro to the game and the team.
- **Warm-up**
- **Game 1:** One-Foot Faceoff (see page 121)
- **Skill Development of skating with stick**
- **Game 2:** Be Ready (see page 120)
- **Cool-down and Review**

Practice 2

- **Purpose:** Lateral skating
- **Warm-up**
- **Game 1:** Freeze Tag (see page 119)
- **Skill Development of skating agility and edges**
- **Game 2:** Freeze Tag (see page 119)
- **Cool-down and Review**

Practice 3

- **Purpose:** Puckhandling
- **Warm-up**
- **Game 1:** King of the Circle (see page 142)
- **Skill Development of creative puckhandling**
- **Game 2:** King of the Circle (see page 142)
- **Cool-down and Review**

Practice 4

- **Purpose:** Advanced shooting
- **Warm-up**
- **Game 1:** Five Prime Shooting (see page 158)
- **Skill Development of shooting; slapshot and snapshot**
- **Game 2:** Five Prime Shooting (see page 158)
- **Cool-down and Review**

Practice 5

- **Purpose:** Advanced passing
- **Warm-up**

- **Game 1:** Flipper (see page 153)
- **Skill Development flip pass**
- **Game 2:** Flipper (see page 153)
- **Cool-down and Review**

Practice 6

- **Purpose:** Advanced backward skating
- **Warm-up**
- **Game 1:** Backward Blitz (see page 137)
- **Skill development of backward skating:** backward one foot stops, T-push, V-stop
- **Game 2:** Backward Blitz (see page 137)
- **Cool-down and Review**

Practice 7

- **Purpose:** Basic checking
- **Warm-up**
- **Game 1:** No Man's Land (see page 165)
- **Skill Development for Body Checking**
- **Game 2:** No Man's Land (see page 165)
- **Cool-down and Review**

Practice 8

- **Purpose:** Puck protection
- **Warm-up**
- **Game 1:** King of the Circle (see page 142)
- **Skill Development for puck protection**
- **Game 2:** King of the Circle (see page 142)
- **Cool-down and Review**

Practice 9

- **Purpose:** Creative puckhandling
- **Warm-up**
- **Game 1:** 10-Yard War (see page 106)
- **Skill Development for puckhandling under pressure**

- **Game 2:** 10-Yard War (see page 106)
- **Cool-down and Review**

Practice 10

- **Purpose:** Backhand shooting and passing
- **Warm-up**
- **Game 1:** Backhand Barrage (see page 151)
- **Skills Development:** for backhand 3 v 3 offensive strategy
- **Game:** Scrimmage
- **Cool-down and Review**

Practice 11

- **Purpose:** Defense
- **Warm-up**
- **Game 1:** Backhand Barrage (see page 151)
- **Skill review for stick checking and defensive positioning**
- **Game 2:** Backhand Barrage (see page 151)
- **Cool-down and Review**

Practice 12

- **Purpose:** Basic checking
- **Warm-up**
- **Game 1:** The Long Skate (see page 163)
- **Skill Development for stick checking**
- **Game 2:** The Long Skate (see page 163)
- **Cool-down and Review**

Practice 13

- **Purpose:** Checking
- **Warm-up**
- **Game 1:** Tight Checking (see page 164)
- **Skill Development stick checking and defensive positioning**
- **Game:** Scrimmage
- **Cool-down and Review**

Practice 14

- ⊙ **Purpose:** Rebound Skills
- ⊙ **Warm-up**
- ⊙ **Game 1:** Burn and Crash (see page 127)
- ⊙ **Skill Development for stopping and rebound skills**
- ⊙ **Game 2:** Burn and Crash (see page 127)
- ⊙ **Cool-down and Review**

Hockey Season Plan for 12- to 14-Year-Olds

At this stage players are refining the skills they have learned from past years. This season plan builds upon the previous one and adds a few new skills, including body checking and rebounding.

Practice 1

- ⊙ **Purpose:** Intro to the game and the team
- ⊙ **Warm-up**
- ⊙ **Game 1:** Get Up and Go (see page 122)
- ⊙ **Skill Development of crossovers and tight turns**
- ⊙ **Game 2:** Get Up and Go (see page 122)
- ⊙ **Cool-down and Review**

Practice 2

- ⊙ **Purpose:** Lateral skating
- ⊙ **Warm-up**
- ⊙ **Game 1:** Freeze Tag (see page 119)
- ⊙ **Skill Development of skating agility and edges**
- ⊙ **Game 2:** Freeze Tag (see page 119)
- ⊙ **Cool-down and Review**

Practice 3

- ⊙ **Purpose:** Puckhandling
- ⊙ **Warm-up**
- ⊙ **Game 1:** 10-Yard War (see page 106)
- ⊙ **Skill Development of creative puckhandling (dekes and fakes)**

- **Game 2:** 10-Yard War (see page 106)
- **Cool-down and Review**

Practice 4

- **Purpose:** Advanced shooting
- **Warm-up**
- **Game 1:** Five Prime Shooting (see page 158)
- **Skill Development of shooting:** slapshot and snapshot
- **Game 2:** Five Prime Shooting (see page 158)
- **Cool-down and Review**

Practice 5

- **Purpose:** Advanced passing
- **Warm-up**
- **Game 1:** One Touch (see page 152)
- **Skill Development of passing game (give and go, drop passes, breakout passes)**
- **Game 2:** One Touch (see page 152)
- **Cool-down and Review**

Practice 6

- **Purpose:** Advanced backward skating
- **Warm-up**
- **Game 1:** Backward Blitz (see page 137)
- **Skill development of backward skating:** backward V-stop, pivoting
- **Game 2:** Backward Blitz (see page 137)
- **Cool-down and Review**

Practice 7

- **Purpose:** Advanced checking
- **Warm-up**
- **Game 1:** No Man's Land (see page 165)
- **Skill Development for checking:** angling the opponent, time and space, legal body checking

- **Game 2:** No Man's Land (see page 165)
- **Cool-down and Review**

Practice 8

- **Purpose:** Shooting
- **Warm-up**
- **Game 1:** Coaches' Choice (see page 159)
- **Skill Development for scoring:** screening, going to the net, and shot selection
- **Game 2:** Coaches' Choice (see page 159)
- **Cool-down and Review**

Practice 9

- **Purpose:** Passing
- **Warm-up**
- **Game 1:** Monkey in the Middle (see page 149)
- **Skill Development for decision making in passing**
- **Game 2:** Monkey in the Middle (see page 149)
- **Cool-down and Review**

Practice 10

- **Purpose:** Puck Handling
- **Warm-up**
- **Game 1:** Fox and the Hounds (see page 143)
- **Skill Development for speed carrying**
- **Game 2:** Fox and the Hounds (see page 143)
- **Cool-down and Review**

Practice 11

- **Purpose:** Defense
- **Warm-up**
- **Game 1:** Backhand Barrage (see page 151)
- **Skill review for stick checking and defensive positioning**
- **Game 2:** Backhand Barrage (see page 151)
- **Cool-down and Review**

Practice 12

- ○ **Purpose:** Turning under pressure
- ○ **Warm-up**
- ○ **Game 1:** Four-Goal Gauntlet (see page 130)
- ○ **Skill Development for turning and pivoting under pressure**
- ○ **Game 2:** Four-Goal Gauntlet (see page 130)
- ○ **Cool-down and Review**

Practice 13

- ○ **Purpose:** Passing and shooting
- ○ **Warm-up**
- ○ **Game 1:** Coaches' Choice (see page 159)
- ○ **Skill Development for offensive movement:** outnumbering, entering the zone, and regrouping
- ○ **Game 2:** Coaches' Choice (see page 159)
- ○ **Cool-down and Review**

Practice 14

- ○ **Purpose:** Rebound skills
- ○ **Warm-up**
- ○ **Game 1:** Burn and Crash (see page 127)
- ○ **Skill Development for stopping and rebound skills**
- ○ **Game:** Scrimmage
- ○ **Cool-down and Review**

Injury Report

Name of athlete _____

Date _____

Time _____

First aider (name) _____

Cause of injury _____

_____

Type of injury _____

Anatomical area involved _____

Extent of injury _____

_____

_____

First aid administered _____

_____

_____

Other treatment administered _____

_____

_____

_____

Referral action _____

_____

_____

_____

_____

First aider (signature)

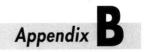

Emergency Information Card

Athlete's name _____ Age _____

Address _____

Phone _____ S.S.# _____

Sport _____

List two persons to contact in case of emergency:

Parent or guardian's name _____

Address _____

Home phone _____ Work phone _____

Second person's name _____

Address _____

Home phone _____ Work phone _____

Relationship to athlete _____

Insurance co. _____ Policy # _____

Physician's name _____ Phone _____

IMPORTANT

Is your child allergic to any drugs? _____ If so, what? _____

Does your child have any other allergies? (e.g., bee stings, dust) _____

Does your child have _____ asthma, _____ diabetes, or _____ epilepsy?

Is your child on any medication? _____ If so, what? _____

Does your child wear contacts? _____

Is there anything else we should know about your child's health or physical condition? If yes, please explain. _____

_____

_____

_____

_____

_____   _____
Signature   Date

Emergency Response Card

Information for emergency call
(Be prepared to give this information to the EMS dispatcher.)

1. Location _____

    Street address _____

    City or town _____

    Directions (cross streets, landmarks, etc.) _____

    _____

    _____ .

2. Telephone number from which call is being made _____

3. Caller's name _____

4. What happened _____

    _____

    _____

    _____

    _____

    _____

5. How many persons injured _____

6. Condition of victim(s) _____

7. Help (first aid) being given _____

    _____

    _____

    _____

Note: Do not hang up first. Let the EMS dispatcher hang up first.